BLOOM
Founded by | arihant

Olympiad ACE

A Comprehensive Practice Book

for School Olympiads & Talent Search Exams

SOCIAL STUDIES

Class 10

by

Adhishree Neurgaonkar

Olympiad ACE

BLOOM

Bloom Cap Edu Ventures Pvt. Ltd.

卐 **Administrative & Production Office**

'Ramchhaya' 4577/15, Agarwal Road, Darya Ganj, New Delhi -110002
Tele: 011- 47630600, 43518550

卐 **PRICE** : ₹125.00

Published by Arihant Publications (I) Ltd.

For further information about the books log on to www.bloomcap.org

Follow us on

Preface

"Future belongs to those Who prepares for it today"

School Olympiads are National & International level competitions conducted by different Government, Non-Government & Educational Organisations with the purpose of making the children ready to face competitive exams.

The challenging Questions asked in Olympiads motivate them to learn more & more and bring out the best results with improved academic performance. The Awards & Scholarship offered by Olympiads motivate children to aspire & strive for doing better and emerge out to be the best.

Social Studies Olympiads

Social Studies provides students with a comprehensive understanding of society, politics, economics and history. Studying Social Studies helps students understand the complexities of society, and prepares them for careers in fields such as public service, education, law, journalism, and research.

Social Studies Olympiads are meant to develop students' interest towards this vital subject.

'Bloom Social Studies Olympiad Study Book Class 10' is a perfect resource to Study & Practice for Olympiad Exams and other National & State Level Talent Search Exams & Other Competitions.

Some Special Features of Bloom Social Studies Olympiad Study Books are;

- Complete coverage of all the aspects of History, Geography and Civics.
- Chapterwise Exercises having different types of Objective Questions at par with the Olympiad Level.
- Olympiad Pattern Practice Sets at the end.

This book is prepared by Expert Panel with the utmost care, still if you have any suggestions regarding its improvement then feel free to contact us at support@bloomcap.org. We will try to inculcate your suggestions in the further editions.

Contents

Chapter 01

Rise of Nationalism in Europe

MCQs 1 Mark Questions

1. 'The Dream of Worldwide Democratic and Social Republics - The Pact Between Nations' is a print, prepared by Frederic Sorrieu. This print is prepared in which of the following years?
   (a) 1868 (b) 1838
   (c) 1848 (d) 1948

2. Which newly designed flag was chosen to replace the formal flag 'Royal Standard' in France?
   (a) Red Cross (b) White Saltire
   (c) Tricolour (d) Union Jack

3. Who designed the cover of a German Almanac in 1798 CE?
   (a) Andreas Rebmann
   (b) Michel Alberganti
   (c) Émilien Amaury
   (d) Marjorie Alessandrini

4. The Napoleonic Code abolished the feudal system and freed peasants from serfdom and manorial dues. What does the term serfdom imply?
   (a) A system where farmers were forced to pay high taxes.
   (b) A system where farmers were forced to live and work under feudal lords.
   (c) A system where farmers were forced to sell their farming lands.
   (d) A system where farmers were forced to sell their produce at nominal rates.

5. The Estates General was elected by the body of active citizens and it was renamed as ....
   (a) State Assembly
   (b) National Assembly
   (c) Republican Assembly
   (d) Civil Assembly

6. Who gave the following definition of a nation state?
   'A nation is the culmination of a long past of endeavours, sacrifice and devotion. A nation is large scale solidarity, its existence is a daily plebiscite.'
   (a) Wolfe Tone (b) Napoleon
   (c) Giuseppe Mazzini (d) Ernest Renan

7. Complete the given analogy.
   Language of Bohemia region : German : : Language of Galicia region : ?
   (a) Spanish (b) Polish
   (c) French (d) Magyar

8. In the image given below, ... is represented as a postman on his way back to France after he lost the battle of .... in 1813.

(a) Napoleon, Vienna
(b) Giuseppe Mazzini, Brussels
(c) Karol Kurspinski, Poland
(d) Napoleon, Leipzig

9. After the defeat of Napoleon in 1815, European government were inspired by a spirit of which of the following?

(a) Liberation (b) Conservatism
(c) Socialism (d) Capitalism

10. What was the provision of 'Treaty of Vienna'?

(a) German confederation of 48 states, that had been set up by Napoleon was not affected by the treaty.
(b) A series of states were set up on the boundaries of France to prevent it expansion in future.
(c) Belgium lost the territories which it had annexed under Napoleon.
(d) In the East, Russia was given part of Hungary.

11. Who among the following led the movement to unify the regions of Italy, but he was neither a revolutionary nor a democrat?

(a) Otto von Bismarck
(b) Count Camillo de Cavour
(c) Victor Emmanuel II
(d) Friedrich Wilhelm IV

12. The July Revolution started an uprising in ...., which led to separation of .... from United Kingdom of the Netherlands.

(a) Brussels, Belgium (b) Belgium, France
(c) Brussels, Rome (d) Vienna, Belgium

13. Complete the given analogy.
1789 : French Revolution initiated : : ? : Greece gained independence

(a) 1848 (b) 1832
(c) 1826 (d) 1837

14.

Which among the following aspects best signifies the above image in 1848 in France?

(a) Peasant uprising
(b) Massacre at Chios
(c) Hall of Versailles
(d) Frankfurt Parliament

15. What did Liberal Nationalism meant for the new middle classes in early 19th century?

(a) Liberalism stood for freedom for the individual and equality of all before the law.
(b) Liberalism stood for the freedom of markets and the abolition of state-imposed restrictions on the movement of goods and capital.
(c) Liberalism stood for freedom of choice of religion.
(d) Liberalism stood for freedom of movement from one place to another.

16.

In the given image, the postage stamp of 1850, with the figure of Marianne represents the Republic of which of the following?

(a) Germany (b) Italy
(c) France (d) Scotland

17.

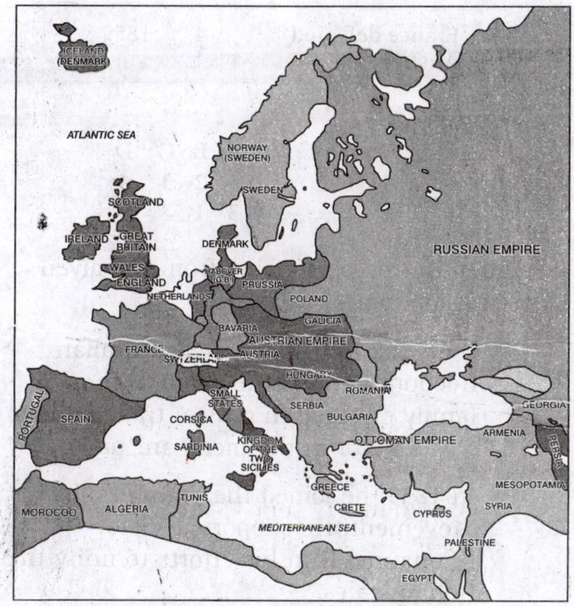

What does the map given above indicates?

(a) Europe after the Unification of Italy
(b) Europe after the French Revolution
(c) Europe after the Treaty of Versailles
(d) Europe after the Congress of Vienna

18. The ....was a region of geographical and ethnic variation comprising modern-day Romania, Bulgaria, Albania, Greece, Macedonia, Croatia, Bosnia-Herzegovina,Slovenia, Serbia and Montenegro whose inhabitants were broadly known as the Slavs.

(a) Balkans (b) Eurasia
(c) Atlanta (d) Magyars

MCQs 2 Marks Questions

19. Identify the incorrectly matched pair.

(a)	Giuseppe Mazzini	–	Formed the secret society 'Young Italy'.
(b)	Giuseppe Garibaldi	–	Participated in republican uprising in Piedmont.
(c)	CM Cavour	–	Succeeded in defeating Prussian forces
(d)	Wolfe Tone	–	Led a revolt against British

20. Arrange the following events in a chronological order.

I. Integration of Italy
II. Greek struggle for independence initiated
III. Unification of Germany
IV. Agreement on Vienna peace settlement

Codes

(a) I, IV, II, III (b) IV, II, III, I
(c) IV, II, I, III (d) I, II, III, IV

21. There are two statements marked as Assertion (A) and Reason (R). Mark your answer as per the codes given below.

Assertion (A) In January 1987, the Prussian king William I was proclaimed German empire in a ceremony held at Versailles.

Reason (R) The nation building process in Germany had demonstrated the dominance of Prussian state power.

Codes

(a) Both A and R are true and R is the correct explanation of A
(b) Both A and R are true, but R is not the correct explanation of A
(c) A is true, but R is false
(d) R is true, but A is false

22. Consider the following statements.

I. During the 19th century, nationalism emerged as a force in Europe.

II. Romanticism was cultural movement that tried to create a sense of collective heritage as a basis of a nation.

III. During the middle of the 19th century, Italy was divided into two states.

IV. Ireland was forcibly incorporated in the United Kingdom of Britain in 1801.

Which of the above statements is/are not correct?

(a) I and II (b) Only III
(c) I, III and IV (d) All of these

23. Read the following statements and select which ones are true (T) and which ones are false (F).

I. The monarchial type of government was functioning in France before the revolution of 1789.

II. The Act of Union between Scotland and England resulted in the formation of the kingdom of Great Britain.

III. Many regions like Italy, Germany, Ireland, Poland, Prussia and the Ottoman empire has witnessed the age of revolution between 1830 to 1848.

IV. The kingdom of Netherlands, which included Belgium was set up in the South and Genoa was added to Piedmont in the South.

Codes

	I	II	III	IV
(a)	T	F	T	T
(b)	F	T	F	T
(c)	T	T	F	F
(d)	T	F	F	T

24. Match the following.

List I	List II
A. English poet Lord Byron died	1. 1707
B. The Act of Union	2. 1861
C. Victor Emmanuel II became king of Italy	3. 1824
D. France defeated Austria	4. 1859

Codes

	A	B	C	D
(a)	4	2	3	1
(b)	1	2	3	4
(c)	4	3	2	1
(d)	3	1	2	4

25. Identify the personality from the given information.

- He is the most celebrated of Italian freedom fighters. He came from a family engaged in coastal trade and was a sailor in the merchant navy.
- In 1833, he joined the Young Italy Movement. He supported Victor Emmanuel II in his efforts to unify the Italian states.

(a) Giuseppe Mazzini
(b) Karol Kurspinski
(c) Napolheon
(d) Garibaldi Mazzini

Darken your choice with HB Pencil

1.	ⓐ ⓑ ⓒ ⓓ	6.	ⓐ ⓑ ⓒ ⓓ	11.	ⓐ ⓑ ⓒ ⓓ	16.	ⓐ ⓑ ⓒ ⓓ	21.	ⓐ ⓑ ⓒ ⓓ
2.	ⓐ ⓑ ⓒ ⓓ	7.	ⓐ ⓑ ⓒ ⓓ	12.	ⓐ ⓑ ⓒ ⓓ	17.	ⓐ ⓑ ⓒ ⓓ	22.	ⓐ ⓑ ⓒ ⓓ
3.	ⓐ ⓑ ⓒ ⓓ	8.	ⓐ ⓑ ⓒ ⓓ	13.	ⓐ ⓑ ⓒ ⓓ	18.	ⓐ ⓑ ⓒ ⓓ	23.	ⓐ ⓑ ⓒ ⓓ
4.	ⓐ ⓑ ⓒ ⓓ	9.	ⓐ ⓑ ⓒ ⓓ	14.	ⓐ ⓑ ⓒ ⓓ	19.	ⓐ ⓑ ⓒ ⓓ	24.	ⓐ ⓑ ⓒ ⓓ
5.	ⓐ ⓑ ⓒ ⓓ	10.	ⓐ ⓑ ⓒ ⓓ	15.	ⓐ ⓑ ⓒ ⓓ	20.	ⓐ ⓑ ⓒ ⓓ	25.	ⓐ ⓑ ⓒ ⓓ

Chapter 02

Nationalism in India

MCQs 1 Mark Questions

1. When did Gandhiji led the satyagraha against racist laws that denied Rights to Non-whites in South Africa?
(a) 13th April, 1913
(b) 6th November, 1913
(c) 18th October, 1892
(d) 8th November, 1912

2. Gandhiji in 1919, decided to launch a nationwide satyagraha against the proposed ....
(a) Rowlatt Act
(b) Indian Emigration Act
(c) East India Company Act
(d) Indian Police Act

3. Council elections were boycotted while Non-Cooperation Movement was in full swing. In which provinces of British India, this election was not boycotted?
(a) Madras (b) United Provinces
(c) Surat (d) Mysore

4. When did the Congress passed the resolution in its Calcutta Session, to start a Non-Cooperation Movement in support of Khilafat and Swaraj?
(a) 1921 (b) 1920 (c) 1922 (d) 1921

5. What was the motive of Mahatma Gandhi behind Khilafat Movement?
(a) Uniting the communities of Hindus and Muslims.
(b) Initiating the Swaraj Movement.
(c) Uniting Sikhs, Parsis, Muslims and Hindus.
(d) Starting the Salt March

6. What does Gandhiji's method of movement and protest based on truth and non-violence called 'satyagraha'?
(a) Satyagraha suggested that if the struggle was against injustice, then physical force was not necessary to fight the oppressor.
(b) The satyagrahi could win the battle through non-violence. This could be done by appealing to the conscience of the oppressor.
(c) Both (a) and (b)
(d) None of the above

7. Who among the following leaders was not the part of the Khilafat Committee?
(a) Hakim Ajmal Khan
(b) Maulana Azad
(c) Hasrat Mohani
(d) Khan Abdul Ghaffar Khan

8. Identify the movement which was adopted by the Congress in 1920, during the Nagpur conference. This movement involved boycott of British goods and promoting the native cottage industries.
(a) Khilafat Movement
(b) Non-Cooperation Movement
(c) Civil Disobedience Movement
(d) Satyagraha Movement

9. Who among the following was the head of Oudh Kisan Sabha?
(a) Motilal Nehru
(b) Mahatma Gandhi
(c) Jawaharlal Nehru
(d) Deen Dayal Upadhyaya

10. According to which act, plantation workers were not permitted to leave the tea gardens without permission?
(a) Inland Emigration Act
(b) East India Company Act
(c) Indian Police Act
(d) Plantation Workers Act

11. Complete the given analogy.
Chauri Chaura incident : 1922 : : Formation of Swaraj Party : ?
(a) 1921 (b) 1922 (c) 1923 (d) 1924

12. What was the main objective behind the formation of Simon Commission?
(a) To control the mass movements in India.
(b) To check the general elections.
(c) To appoint the Indian leaders in civil services.
(d) To check the functioning of constitutional system.

13. Hindustan Socialist Republican Army (HSRA) was founded at a meeting in Delhi. Its leaders were Bhagat Singh, ………….. and Ajoy Ghosh.
(a) Raj Guru
(b) Subhash Chandra Bose
(c) Lala Lajpat Rai (d) Jatin Das

14. 

This most famous picture is taken during which of the following nationalist movements?
(a) Khilafat Movement (b) Salt March
(c) Swaraj Movement (d) Rowlatt Act

15. Whose arrest caused the severe violence in all over India which made the Mahatma Gandhi obliged to sign Gandhi-Irwin Pact?
(a) Netaji Subhash Chandra Bose
(b) Jawaharlal Nehru
(c) Rabindranath Tagore
(d) Khan Abdul Ghaffar Khan

16. What is not the interest social groups behind supporting Swaraj?
(a) Jats of Uttar Pradesh will remove intensive farming techniques.
(b) Patidards of Gujarat will abolish high revenues.
(c) Business class will liberalise business doing technique.
(d) Poor peasantry will abolish high rents.

17. Which president of Muslim league demanded the separate electorates for Muslims in 1930?
(a) Mohammad Ali Jauhar
(b) Zafar Ali Khan
(c) Syed Nabiullah (d) Muhammad Iqbal

18. Who designed the Swaraj Flag in 1921, which had a tricolour with a spinning wheel in the centre?
(a) Bankim Chandra Chattopadhyay
(b) Rabindranath Tagore
(c) Mahatma Gandhi
(d) Pingali Venkayya

MCQs 2 Marks Questions

19. Identify the incorrectly matched pair.

Events	Year
(a) Gandhiji organised a satyagraha to support the peasants of the Kheda district of Gujarat –	1917
(b) Mahatma Gandhi went to Ahmedabad to organise a Satyagraha Movement amongst cotton mill workers –	1918
(c) Gandhiji travelled to Champaran in Bihar to inspire the peasants to struggle against the oppressive plantation system –	1916
(d) Mahatma Gandhi returned to India from South Africa –	1915

20. Consider the following statements regarding Rowlatt Act, 1919 and identify the correct option.

I. According to this act, the political prisoners could be detained in prison for two years without any trial.

II. This act was passed through the Imperial Legislative Council in 1919 and was hugely supported by the Indian members.

III. Martial law was imposed in Champaran and the command of area was given to General Dyer.

Codes

(a) Both I and II (b) Only III
(c) Only I (d) Both I and III

21. Arrange the following events in a chronological order.

I. Incident of Chauri-Chaura
II. Arrival of Simon Commission
III. Signing of Poona Pact
IV. Formation of Indian Chamber of Commerce and Industries

Codes

(a) IV, I, III, II (b) I, IV, II, III
(c) III, I, II, IV (d) I, III, II, IV

22. Match the following.

List I	List II
A. 1921	1. Non-Cooperation Movement
B. 1924	2. Khilafat Committee Formation
C. 1919	3. Second Round Table Conference
D. 1932	4. Death of Alluri Sitaram Raju

Codes

	A	B	C	D		A	B	C	D
(a)	2	3	4	1	(b)	2	1	4	3
(c)	4	3	2	1	(d)	1	4	2	3

23. There are two statements marked as Assertion (A) and Reason (R). Mark your answer as per the codes given below.

Assertion (A) The Chauri-Chaura incident occurred in Gorakhpur district of Uttar Pradesh.

Reason (R) Large number of people participated in Non-Cooperation Movement.

Codes

(a) Both A and R are true and R is correct explanation of A
(b) Both A and R are true, but R is not the correct explanation of A
(c) A is true, but R is false
(d) A is false, but R is true

24. Read the following statements and select which ones are true (T) and which ones are false (F).

I. The picture of Bharat Mata is drawn by Abanindranath Tagore.

II. Alongwith 77 followers, Gandhiji started his salt march from Sabarmati Ashram on 12th March, 1932 for Dandi.

III. Vallabhbhai Patel led the Peasant Movement in Bardoli in 1928.

Codes

	I	II	III		I	II	III
(a)	T	T	T	(b)	F	T	F
(c)	T	F	T	(d)	F	T	T

25. Read the following passage and answer the following question.

The effects of this movement on the economic front were more dramatic. In many places, merchants and traders refused to trade in foreign goods or finance foreign trade. As the boycott movement spread, and people began discarding imported clothes and wearing only Indian ones, production of Indian textile mills and handlooms went up.

Which of the following movements has been discussed in the above passage?

(a) Non-Cooperation Movement
(b) Swaraj Movement
(c) Rowlatt Act
(d) Civil Disobedience Movement

26. Identify the personality from the given information.

- He demanded reserved seats in educational institutions and a separate electorate that would choose Dalit members for Legislative Councils.
- He organised the Dalits into the Depressed Class Association in 1930.

(a) Mahatma Gandhi
(b) Deen Dayal Upadhyaya
(c) BR Ambedkar
(d) Jawaharlal Nehru

27. Identify the features marked as A and B on the given map with the help of the following information.

A. The centre/place of calling off/withdrawing of the Non-Cooperation Movement.

B. The place is known for the movement of Indigo peasants during the British period.

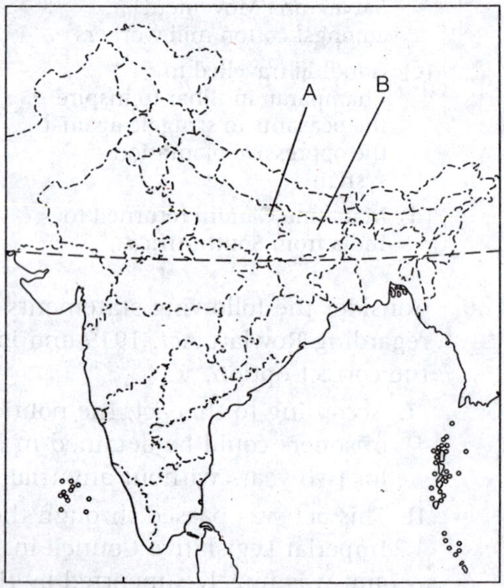

	A	B
(a)	Chauri-Chaura	Champaran
(b)	Champaran	Chauri-Chaura
(c)	Oudh	Patna
(d)	Champaran	Patna

Darken your choice with HB Pencil

1.	ⓐ ⓑ ⓒ ⓓ	6.	ⓐ ⓑ ⓒ ⓓ	11.	ⓐ ⓑ ⓒ ⓓ	16.	ⓐ ⓑ ⓒ ⓓ	21.	ⓐ ⓑ ⓒ ⓓ	26.	ⓐ ⓑ ⓒ ⓓ
2.	ⓐ ⓑ ⓒ ⓓ	7.	ⓐ ⓑ ⓒ ⓓ	12.	ⓐ ⓑ ⓒ ⓓ	17.	ⓐ ⓑ ⓒ ⓓ	22.	ⓐ ⓑ ⓒ ⓓ	27.	ⓐ ⓑ ⓒ ⓓ
3.	ⓐ ⓑ ⓒ ⓓ	8.	ⓐ ⓑ ⓒ ⓓ	13.	ⓐ ⓑ ⓒ ⓓ	18.	ⓐ ⓑ ⓒ ⓓ	23.	ⓐ ⓑ ⓒ ⓓ		
4.	ⓐ ⓑ ⓒ ⓓ	9.	ⓐ ⓑ ⓒ ⓓ	14.	ⓐ ⓑ ⓒ ⓓ	19.	ⓐ ⓑ ⓒ ⓓ	24.	ⓐ ⓑ ⓒ ⓓ		
5.	ⓐ ⓑ ⓒ ⓓ	10.	ⓐ ⓑ ⓒ ⓓ	15.	ⓐ ⓑ ⓒ ⓓ	20.	ⓐ ⓑ ⓒ ⓓ	25.	ⓐ ⓑ ⓒ ⓓ		

Chapter
03

The Making of a Global World

MCQs 1 Mark Questions

1. Which term is used to describe how trade and technology have made the world into a more connected and interdependent place?

(a) Liberalisation (b) Globalisation
(c) Socialism (d) Proliferation

2. What was not the reason behind travelling of vast distances by travellers, traders, priests and pilgrims?

(a) For religious and spiritual fulfillment
(b) To gain knowledge
(c) To escape from ill treatment
(d) To spread diseases and germs

3. .... was used as a form of currency from Maldives to China and East Africa.

(a) Kenyan Shilling
(b) Rufiyaa
(c) Cowries
(d) Yuan

4.

In which of the following museum this image has been kept?

(a) National Museum
(b) Goa Museum
(c) Chennai Museum
(d) Salar Jung Museum

5. Which of the following foods were not introduced in Europe and Asia after America was discovered by Christopher Columbus?

(a) Sweet potatoes (b) Maize
(c) Onion (d) Chilly

6. In which of the following cities, many expeditions were taken for the search of gold?

(a) Alaska (b) El Dorado
(c) El Salvador (d) Peru

7. The conquest of America was possible through the deadly disease called .... that the Spanish carried on their person.

(a) influenza (b) meales
(c) small pox (d) flu

8. Economists identify three types of movements or flows within international economic exchanges. Which among the following flows was not identified by economists?

(a) Flow of trade (b) Flow of culture
(c) Flow of labour (d) Flow of capital

9. Identify the building shown in the picture below.

(a) East India Company House, London
(b) Calcutta East India House
(c) East India Company, Surat
(d) The Smithfield Club

10. Which of the following is not the effect of Corn Law?
(a) Increasing number of workers needed more homes and settlements.
(b) Capital flowed from financial centers such as America.
(c) Consumption in Britain increased due to decrease in food prices.
(d) By the 1890, a global agricultural economy had developed.

11. What does the given picture signifies?

(a) Indian indentured labour
(b) Emigrant ship leaving for the US
(c) Irish Emigrants
(d) Slaves for sale

12. Name the writer who was descendent of indentured labour migrants and also got Nobel Prize.
(a) VS Naipaul
(b) S Chanderpaul
(c) Ramnaresh Sarwan
(d) Ram Narayan Tiwari

13. Which of the following was riotous carnival held in Trinidad when workers of all races and religions join to celebrate?
(a) Chettiars (b) Hosay
(c) Chutney (d) Rastafarianism

14. Why was/were the First World War also called the first modern industrial war?
(a) Many industries were destroyed in the war.
(b) Soldiers fought with Rifle.
(c) Factory-made guns, tanks and aircrafts were extensively used.
(d) All of the above

15. When did the Great Depression began?
(a) 1829 (b) 1929
(c) 1934 (d) 1922

16. What was the impact of the First World War?
(a) Household incomes declined due to death or the injury of the earning members of the family.
(b) USA became an international creditor by giving huge sum of credit to African and Asian countries.
(c) The wheat exports from Eastern Europe were disrupted during the First World War.
(d) None of the above

17. Who adapted assembly line method for car production in Detroit?
(a) Tata Motors (b) Honda
(c) Toyota Kirloskar (d) Henry Ford

18. During the period of Great Depression, India became an exporter of precious metals like ....

(a) silver
(b) diamond
(c) gold
(d) bronze

19. What was established by the Bretton Wood Conference to deal with external surpluses and deficit of its member nations?

(a) International Monetary Fund
(b) World Bank
(c) UNESCO
(d) International Bank for reconstruction and development

MCQs 2 Marks Questions

20. Consider the following statements regarding Silk routes.

I. Silk routes were existed since before the Christian era and flourished till the 14th century.
II. The silk routes are good example of pre-modern trade and cultural links between distant parts of the world linking Asia with Europe and North Africa.
III. Along the silk routes, the cargoes from China, Indian spices and textiles, gold and bronze from Europe were carried from different parts of the world.

Which of the above statements is/are correct?

(a) Both II and III
(b) Both I and II
(c) Only II
(d) Only III

21. Read the following statements and select which ones are true (T) and which ones are false (F).

I. British forced the farmers of India to produce indigo and opium.
II. The British Government introduced high tarrifs on export of Indian cotton clothes.
III. Opium grown in India was exported to China.
IV. The money earned through opium sale was used by Britain to finance its cotton mills and other industries.

Codes

	I	II	III	IV		I	II	III	IV
(a)	T	F	F	F	(b)	F	F	T	F
(c)	T	T	F	T	(d)	T	F	T	F

22. Arrange the following events in a chronological order.

I. Existence of silk route
II. Potato famine in Ireland
III. Rinderpest arrival in Africa
IV. The First World War

Codes

(a) I, IV, II, III (b) I, II, III, IV
(c) III, IV, I, II (d) I, III, II, IV

23. Match the following.

List I		List II
A. 1914	1.	The First World War started
B. 1921	2.	Indenture labour abolished
C. 1944	3.	International Monetary fund founded
D. 1939	4.	Second World War started

Codes

	A	B	C	D		A	B	C	D
(a)	1	3	2	4	(b)	1	2	3	4
(c)	4	3	2	1	(d)	2	1	3	4

24. There are two statements marked as Assertion (A) and Reason (R). Mark your answer as per the codes given below.

Assertion (A) To deal with external surpluses and deficits a conference was held in July, 1944 at Bretton Woods in New Hampshire, USA.

Reason (R) The world wide spread of MNCs was a notable feature in the 1950s and 1960s as US business expanded worldwide.

Codes

(a) Both A and R are true and R is correct explanation of A

(b) Both A and R are true, but R is not the correct explanation of A

(c) A is true, but R is false

(d) A is false, but R is true

25. Identify the personality from the given information.

- The assembly line method was introduced by this American industrialist. He was also the founder of a important motor company.
- He is famous for inventing a system of mass production with high wages of workers and revolutionising factory production.

(a) Karl Friedrich

(b) August Horch

(c) Henry Ford

(d) Ferdinand Porsche

26. Identify the regions marked as A and B on the map of Africa given below.

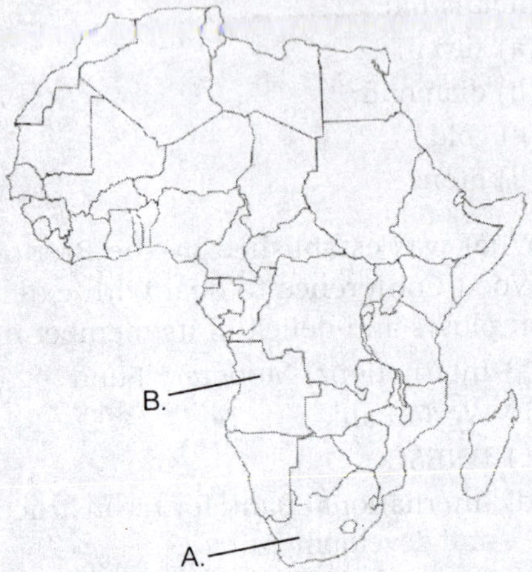

	A	B
(a)	Union of South Africa	Angola
(b)	British Dominion	Portuguese Colony
(c)	Madagascar	Sierra Leone
(d)	Madagascar	Portuguese Colony

27. Fill in the blanks with appropriate words.

The Bretton Woods system inaugurated an era of unprecedented growth of trade and incomes for the ......(I)...... industrial nations and ......(II)...... .

Codes

	I	II
(a)	Eastern	Italy
(b)	Western	Japan
(c)	Northern	Europe
(d)	Southern	Germany

Darken your choice with HB Pencil

1.	ⓐ ⓑ ⓒ ⓓ	6.	ⓐ ⓑ ⓒ ⓓ	11.	ⓐ ⓑ ⓒ ⓓ	16.	ⓐ ⓑ ⓒ ⓓ	21.	ⓐ ⓑ ⓒ ⓓ	26.	ⓐ ⓑ ⓒ ⓓ
2.	ⓐ ⓑ ⓒ ⓓ	7.	ⓐ ⓑ ⓒ ⓓ	12.	ⓐ ⓑ ⓒ ⓓ	17.	ⓐ ⓑ ⓒ ⓓ	22.	ⓐ ⓑ ⓒ ⓓ	27.	ⓐ ⓑ ⓒ ⓓ
3.	ⓐ ⓑ ⓒ ⓓ	8.	ⓐ ⓑ ⓒ ⓓ	13.	ⓐ ⓑ ⓒ ⓓ	18.	ⓐ ⓑ ⓒ ⓓ	23.	ⓐ ⓑ ⓒ ⓓ		
4.	ⓐ ⓑ ⓒ ⓓ	9.	ⓐ ⓑ ⓒ ⓓ	14.	ⓐ ⓑ ⓒ ⓓ	19.	ⓐ ⓑ ⓒ ⓓ	24.	ⓐ ⓑ ⓒ ⓓ		
5.	ⓐ ⓑ ⓒ ⓓ	10.	ⓐ ⓑ ⓒ ⓓ	15.	ⓐ ⓑ ⓒ ⓓ	20.	ⓐ ⓑ ⓒ ⓓ	25.	ⓐ ⓑ ⓒ ⓓ		

Chapter
04

The Age of Industrialisation

MCQs 1 Mark Questions

1. Modernisation began with age of industrialisation in ………………… .

(a) America (b) Asia

(c) Europe (d) Africa

2. What does the term proto-industrialisation stand for?

(a) Period before or beginning of industrialisation.

(b) Period just after the process of industrialisation.

(c) Period before the process of development.

(d) Period at the phase of industrialisation.

3. Which of the following is/are not the feature(s) of the proto-industrialisation system?

(a) The proto-industrial system was a network of commercial exchange and was controlled by the merchants.

(b) Income from proto-industrial production supplemented feudal lord's income from peasants.

(c) The good were produced by a vast number of producers working within their family firms instead of factories.

(d) All of the above

4. When was the first factory in England established?

(a) 1734 (b) 1730 (c) 1731 (d) 1729

5. Which industry was the most important industry in the late 18th century?

(a) Jute industry (b) Spinning industry

(c) Opium industry (d) Cotton industry

6.

When did the illustration given above was published?

(a) 1904 (b) 1911 (c) 1901 (d) 1905

7. ……… machine was devised by James Hargreaves in 1764, which speeded up the spinning process and reduced labour demands.

(a) Spinning Jenny (b) Spinning Mule

(c) Spinning Carding (d) Spinning Frame

8. What was the condition of workers during industrialisation?
(a) Many job seekers had to wait for weeks spending nights under bridges and in night shelters set up by private individuals.
(b) The possibility of getting a job depended on the mental capacity and strong physical ability.
(c) The income of workers depended on the number of days of their work.
(d) None of the above

9. Identify the ports that grew after the European companies gained power in trade.
(a) Surat and Hoogly
(b) Madras and Masulipatnam
(c) Bombay and Calcutta
(d) Kandla and Visakhapatnam

10. The East India Company started appointing Gomasthas to supervise weavers, collect supplies and examine the quality of clothes. What does the term Gomasthas indicate?
(a) Forced labours (b) Indentured labours
(c) Paid labours (d) Supervisors

11. Which of the following is not an European managing agency who controlled large sector of Indian industries during the First World War?
(a) Bird Heiglers and Company
(b) East India Company
(c) Andrew Yule
(d) Jardine Skinner

12. Who amongst the following industrialists began selling cloth in India with labels on cloth bundles?
(a) Manchester industrialists
(b) Yorkshire industrialists
(c) Lancashire industrialists
(d) Glasgow industrialists

13. What problems was/were faced by the cotton weavers in India?
(a) Their export market were collapsed.
(b) The local market shrank.
(c) They did not get sufficient supply of raw cotton.
(d) All of the above

14. Find the incorrect option.
(a) Earliest factories started in England in 1730.
(b) James Watt patents the Steam Engine in 1781.
(c) In 1855, first jute mill came up in Punjab.
(d) By 1874, the first spinning and weaving of Madras began production.

15. Who among the following businessmen set up the first Indian Jute Mill in Calcutta in 1917?
(a) GD Birla
(b) Seth Hukumchand
(c) Dwarkanath Tagore
(d) JN Tata

16. Why the Industrial growth was/were slow during the First World War?
(a) British mills were busy with war production.
(b) Manchester imports into India declined.
(c) Indian factories were also busy with the production of items needed for war.
(d) All of the above

17. Sometimes .... became a medium of the national message of Swadeshi which guaranteed the quality of good.
(a) promotion
(b) selling
(c) advertisement
(d) patriotism

18. Complete the given analogy.
First Iron and Steel works was set up : 1912 : : Elgin Mill was started in Kanpur :?
(a) 1906 (b) 1860
(c) 1865 (d) 1964

19. Which of the following Indian kings is depicted in this Manchester label?

(a) Sher Shah Suri
(b) Maharaja Ranjit Singh
(c) Maharaja Kharak Singh
(d) Babur

MCQs 2 Marks Questions

20. Consider the following statements with reference to the World Trade during the 17th and 18th century.
I. In the towns, urban crafts and trade guilds were very powerful. Different guilds were granted the rights of production and trade for a specific product by the rulers.
II. With the expansion of world trade and the acquisition of colonies of different parts in the world, the demand for goods began growing.
III. In the countryside, the income of poor peasants was very meagre.

Which of the above statement are correct?
(a) Both I and II (b) Both II and III
(c) Both I and III (d) All of these

21. There are two statements marked as Assertion (A) and Reason (R). Mark your answer as per the codes given below.
Assertion (A) The period of industrialisation before the first factories came up in Europe is termed as proto-industrialisation.
Reason (R) This period was marked by merchants from towns getting products made in villages.
Codes
(a) Both A and R are true and R is the correct explanation of A
(b) Both A and R are true, but R is not the correct explanation of A
(c) A is true, but R is false
(d) A is false, but R is true

22. Read the following statements and select which ones are true (T) and which ones are false (F).
I. The East India Company appointed Gomasthas to supervise weavers, collect supplies and examine the quality of cloth.
II. In Victorian Britain, the bourgeoisie class preferred machine made goods.
III. Richard Ark Wright is credited to create the cotton mill.
IV. The introduction of the fly shuttle (a mechanical device used for weaving) during the second decade of the 20th century helped in improving production of the Indian handloom industry.

Codes

	I	II	III	IV		I	II	III	IV
(a)	T	T	T	F	(b)	F	T	F	T
(c)	T	F	T	T	(d)	T	F	T	F

23. Fill in the blanks by choosing the most appropriate options.

The first cotton mill was set up in 1854 in ......(I)..... and the first jute mill was set up in 1855 in Bengal. In North India, Elgin Mill was started in ......(II)....... in 1860s and a year later, first cotton mill was setup in Ahmedabad. By 1874, the first spinning and weaving mill of ......(III)...... began production.

Codes

	I	II	III
(a)	Bombay	Kanpur	Madras
(b)	Madras	Bombay	Kanpur
(c)	Bombay	Kanpur	Bengaluru
(d)	Chennai	Kanpur	Madras

24. Match the following.

List I (Year)	**List II** (Events)
A. 1730	1. Earliest factories started in England
B. 1781	2. James Watt patents the steam Engine
C. 1771	3. Creation of first cotton mill by R Arkwright
D. 1855	4. First Jute mill came up in Bengal

Codes

	A	B	C	D
(a)	1	2	3	4
(b)	4	2	3	1
(c)	3	2	1	4
(d)	2	3	4	1

25. Read the following passage and answer the following question.

Advertisement, labelling and calendars were used to popularise products by both British and Indian manufactures. Advertisement through newspapers, magazines and hoardings were used by the producers to expand their market. Advertisement makes products appear desirable and necessary.

Which image of a God was most commonly used in advertisement to popularise baby products?

(a) Ram (b) Krishna
(c) Shiva (d) Hanuman

26. Identify the personality by studying the following synopsis.

- He set up the first Iron and Steel works in India at Jamshedpur.
- He was an Indian pioneer industrialist who founded the India's biggest conglomerate company.

(a) JN Tata (b) Naval Tata
(c) Ratanji Tata (d) Ratan Tata

27. What does the given map of India in 1931 indicates?

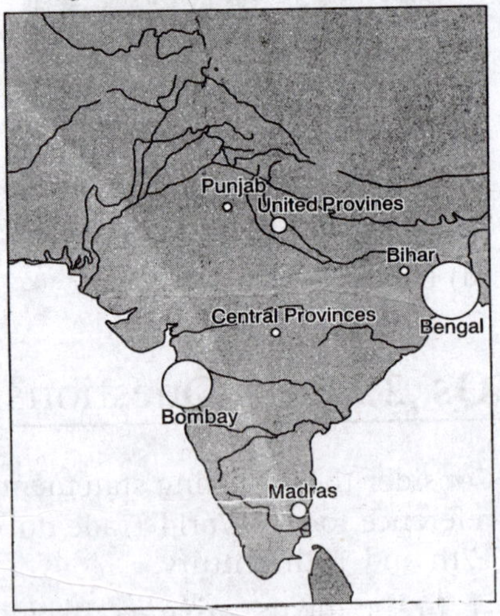

(a) Cotton mills in India
(b) Large scale industries in India
(c) Small scale industries in India
(d) Jute and leather mills in India

Darken your choice with HB Pencil

1. ⓐ ⓑ ⓒ ⓓ	6. ⓐ ⓑ ⓒ ⓓ	11. ⓐ ⓑ ⓒ ⓓ	16. ⓐ ⓑ ⓒ ⓓ	21. ⓐ ⓑ ⓒ ⓓ	26. ⓐ ⓑ ⓒ ⓓ
2. ⓐ ⓑ ⓒ ⓓ	7. ⓐ ⓑ ⓒ ⓓ	12. ⓐ ⓑ ⓒ ⓓ	17. ⓐ ⓑ ⓒ ⓓ	22. ⓐ ⓑ ⓒ ⓓ	27. ⓐ ⓑ ⓒ ⓓ
3. ⓐ ⓑ ⓒ ⓓ	8. ⓐ ⓑ ⓒ ⓓ	13. ⓐ ⓑ ⓒ ⓓ	18. ⓐ ⓑ ⓒ ⓓ	23. ⓐ ⓑ ⓒ ⓓ	
4. ⓐ ⓑ ⓒ ⓓ	9. ⓐ ⓑ ⓒ ⓓ	14. ⓐ ⓑ ⓒ ⓓ	19. ⓐ ⓑ ⓒ ⓓ	24. ⓐ ⓑ ⓒ ⓓ	
5. ⓐ ⓑ ⓒ ⓓ	10. ⓐ ⓑ ⓒ ⓓ	15. ⓐ ⓑ ⓒ ⓓ	20. ⓐ ⓑ ⓒ ⓓ	25. ⓐ ⓑ ⓒ ⓓ	

Chapter 05

Print Culture and the Modern World

MCQs 1 Mark Questions

1. Which among the following countries had the earliest kind of print technology?
(a) China (b) Korea
(c) New Zealand (d) Both (a) and (b)

2. A vast number of text books was printed in China under the sponsorship of the ....
(a) government (b) state
(c) craftsmen (d) imperial state

3. In which of the following years, Buddhist missionaries from China introduced hand printing technology?
(a) 756-760 AD (b) 768-770 AD
(c) 772-779 AD (d) 776-780 AD

4. Which of the following is the oldest Japanese book printed in 868 AD?
(a) Nihongi
(b) The Manusmriti
(c) Buddhist Diamond Sutra
(d) Hokegisho

5. Who returned to Italy and brought the technology of wood block printing from China?
(a) Marco Polo (b) Fa-Hien
(c) Hiuen-Tsang (d) Ferdinand Magellan

6. A parchment made from skin of animals is known as ....
(a) papyrus (b) text
(c) vellum (d) palimpsest

7. When was the Jikji of Korea, the world's oldest existing book on Zex Buddhism printed?
(a) 15th century (b) 17th century
(c) 14th century (d) 12th century

8. Who among the following developed the first printing press in 1430's?
(a) Gutenberg (b) George Eliot
(c) Austen (d) None of these

9. How many sheets were printed by Gutenberg press in one hour on one side?
(a) 230 sheets (b) 240 sheets
(c) 260 sheets (d) 250 sheets

10. Complete the given analogy.
Chapbook : ? : : Almanac : An Astronomical Calendar
(a) Books of poems
(b) Books of Ballads and Folk tales
(c) Summary books of Bible
(d) Romantic novels

11. Who wrote 'Ninety-Five Theses' criticising many of the practices and rituals of the Roman Catholic Church in 1517?
(a) John Calvin (b) Katharina Bora
(c) Martin Luther (d) James Hickey

12. In which of the following years, the children press in France was established?
(a) 1823 (b) 1860 (c) 1857 (d) 1845

13. Who among the following was not the best known women novelists of Europe?
(a) Bronte sisters (b) Jane Austen
(c) George Eliot (d) Doris Lessing

14. The protrait given below is of Johann Gutenberg. Identify the incorrect statement about him.

(a) He knew the art of polishing stones.
(b) He was expert in creating moulds used for making trinkets.
(c) He was a master goldsmith.
(d) None of the above

15. What is known as the doctrine or belief that there is only one God?
(a) Shaivism (b) Henotheism
(c) Monotheism (d) Ulama

16. Why reading of manuscript was not easy in India? Choose the most appropriate reason from the following options.
(a) Manuscript was highly expensive.
(b) Manuscript were widely spread out.
(c) Manuscript were unilingual.
(d) Manuscript were fragile.

17. The first printing press came to ...... with Portuguese missionaries in mid ....
(a) Bengal, 17th century
(b) Goa, 16th century
(c) Madras, 16th century
(d) United Provinces, 15th century

18. Who was the content editor of Bengal Gazette which was a weekly English magazine?
(a) Warren Hastings
(b) Raja Ram Mohan Roy
(c) James Hickey
(d) Anna Winterbottom

19. When was the Deoband Seminary founded in North India, which published thousand of fatwas telling Muslims how to conduct their everyday life and explained the meaning of Islamic doctrines?
(a) 1867 (b) 1848 (c) 1883 (d) 1858

MCQs 2 Marks Questions

20. Consider the following statements regarding the print technology of China and choose the correct statements.

I. Books in China were printed by rubbing paper against the inked surface of wooden blocks.
II. The traditional Chinese Accordion Book was folded and stitched at the middle because both sides of the thin opaque sheets could not be printed.
III. The skilled craftsman could copy the beauty of calligraphy with remarkable accuracy.

Codes
(a) I and III
(b) Both II and III
(c) I and II
(d) All of the above

21. Arrange the following events in a chronological order.

I. Paper reached Europe from China.

II. Buddhist missionaries from China introduced hand printing technology into Japan.

III. Marco Polo brought woodblock printing technology into Europe from China.

IV. Printing done in China by rubbing paper against the inked surface of wooden blocks.

Codes

(a) IV, II, III, I (b) IV, II, I, III

(c) III, II, IV, I (d) II, III, I, IV

22. Identify the personality from the following information.

He was born in 1753 and was widely known for his contributions to an art form called Ukiyo (pictures of the floating world) or depiction of ordinary human experiences, especially urban ones.

(a) Tsutaya Juzaburo (b) Kitagawa Utamaro

(c) Van Gogh (d) Monet

23. There are two statements marked as Assertion (A) and Reason (R). Mark your answer as per the codes given below.

Assertion (A) After the mid of 18th century, women schools were set up in the cities and towns.

Reason (R) Many journals began carrying the writings of women and explained why women should be educated.

Codes

(a) Both A and R are true and R is the correct explanation of A

(b) Both A and R are true, but R is not the correct explanation of A

(c) A is true, but R is false

(d) A is false, but R is true

24. Read the following statements and select which ones are true (T) and which ones are false (F).

I. The first book printed by Gutenberg was Bible.

II. The first printed edition of the Ramcharitmanas of Tulsidas was published in 1819 from Calcutta.

III. In 1576, Menocchio reinterpreted the message of the Bible, but his interpretation made the Roman Catholic Church angry.

Codes

	I	II	III		I	II	III
(a)	F	F	T	(b)	T	F	F
(c)	T	T	T	(d)	F	T	T

25. Match the following.

Year		Event
A. 1930	1.	Calcutta Supreme Court passed regulations to control press freedom
B. 1820	2.	Caricatures and cartoons were published in journals and newspapers commenting on social issues
C. 1850	3.	Bangalore cotton mill workers set up common library to educate themselves
D. 1579	4.	First Tamil book published

Codes

	A	B	C	D		A	B	C	D
(a)	3	1	2	4	(b)	4	2	3	1
(c)	1	2	3	4	(d)	3	2	1	4

Darken your choice with HB Pencil

1.	ⓐ ⓑ ⓒ ⓓ	6.	ⓐ ⓑ ⓒ ⓓ	11.	ⓐ ⓑ ⓒ ⓓ	16.	ⓐ ⓑ ⓒ ⓓ	21.	ⓐ ⓑ ⓒ ⓓ
2.	ⓐ ⓑ ⓒ ⓓ	7.	ⓐ ⓑ ⓒ ⓓ	12.	ⓐ ⓑ ⓒ ⓓ	17.	ⓐ ⓑ ⓒ ⓓ	22.	ⓐ ⓑ ⓒ ⓓ
3.	ⓐ ⓑ ⓒ ⓓ	8.	ⓐ ⓑ ⓒ ⓓ	13.	ⓐ ⓑ ⓒ ⓓ	18.	ⓐ ⓑ ⓒ ⓓ	23.	ⓐ ⓑ ⓒ ⓓ
4.	ⓐ ⓑ ⓒ ⓓ	9.	ⓐ ⓑ ⓒ ⓓ	14.	ⓐ ⓑ ⓒ ⓓ	19.	ⓐ ⓑ ⓒ ⓓ	24.	ⓐ ⓑ ⓒ ⓓ
5.	ⓐ ⓑ ⓒ ⓓ	10.	ⓐ ⓑ ⓒ ⓓ	15.	ⓐ ⓑ ⓒ ⓓ	20.	ⓐ ⓑ ⓒ ⓓ	25.	ⓐ ⓑ ⓒ ⓓ

Chapter 06

Resources and Development

MCQs 1 Mark Questions

1. How do human beings interact with nature?
   (a) Through technology
   (b) Through nurturing environmental resources
   (c) Through industry
   (d) Through experimental advances

2. Which of these resources are based on ownership
   (a) Individual resources
   (b) Abiotic
   (c) Renewable resources
   (d) Potential resources

3. Which of the following pairs is/are incorrect?

(a)	States having coal	–	Jharkhand
(b)	State having abundant water resource	–	Arunachal Pradesh
(c)	State having abundant solar energy	–	Madhya Pradesh
(d)	State/Union Territory having cold desert	–	Ladakh

4. The first International Earth Summit was held in ....
   (a) Tokyo (b) Rio de Janerio
   (c) Paris (d) Moscow

5. Which among the following State(s) of India is/are rich in coal and minerals?
   (a) Jharkhand (b) Chhattisgarh
   (c) Madhya Pradesh (d) All of these

6. Why do we need resource planning?
   (a) Because of enormous diversity in the availability of resources.
   (b) Because we need to think of future generations.
   (c) We need to consider materials in the environment which have the potential to satisfy human needs.
   (d) Because of the need to collect materials and resources, and then using them accordingly.

7. What is essential for sustainable existence of all forms of life?
   (a) Resource extraction
   (b) Resource management
   (c) Resource planning
   (d) Resource generation

8. Area sown more than once in an agricultural year plus net sown area is known as ....

(a) cropped area (b) fallow lands
(c) gross cropped area (d) grazing land

9. Which type of land is left uncultivated for more than five agricultural years?

(a) Fallow land
(b) Barren and wasteland
(c) Culturable wasteland
(d) Grazing land

10. Identify the soil which is more common in Piedmont plains such as Duars, Chos and Terai.

(a) Laterite soil (b) Alluvial soil
(c) Black soil (d) Red soil

11. Identify the type of erosion which is depicted in the picture given below.

(a) Gully erosion (b) Wind erosion
(c) Sheet erosion (d) Glacial erosion

12. Why the lower horizons of the arid soil is occupied by Kankar?

(a) Increase in potash content
(b) Increase in lime, potash and phosphorous content
(c) Increase in calcium content
(d) Increase in phosphorous content

13. What is/are the objective(s) of Agenda 21?

(a) It aims at achieving global sustainable development.
(b) It is an agenda to combat environmental damage, poverty and disease through global cooperation.
(c) It's objective is that every local government should not draw its own local Agenda 21.
(d) Both (a) and (b)

14. How gullies are formed in bad lands?

(a) These are formed when water flows over large areas down a slope.
(b) These are formed when moving wind blows away loose soil of flat lands.
(c) These are formed when running water cuts through soils making deep channels.
(d) These are formed when ploughing is done in a wrong way.

15. Choose the incorrect statement about terrace cultivation.

(a) It is practiced along the line of slope.
(b) It reduces the speed of water.
(c) It is generally done in mountainous areas.
(d) It ultimately reduces soil erosion caused by wind.

16. Identify the correctly matched pair.

(a) Continuous resource – Metal
(b) Recyclable resource – Fossil fuels
(c) Non-recyclable resource – Metals
(d) Potential resource – Wind and solar energy

17. Which of the following is depicted in the given picture?

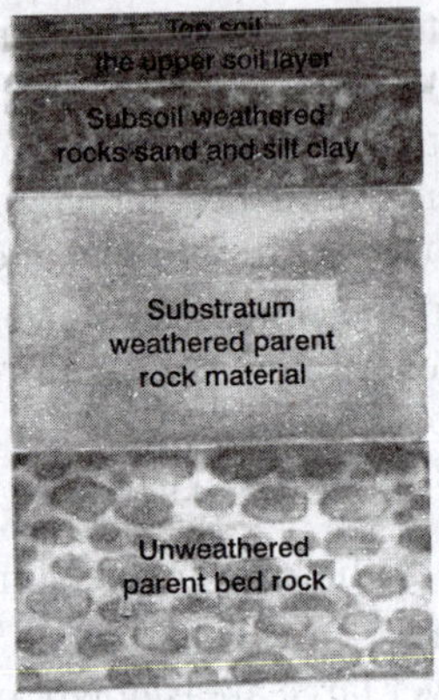

(a) Types of soil
(b) Layers of the Earth
(c) Soil profile
(d) Rock structure

18. The process of transformation of things available in our environment involves an interactive relationship between ...., ... and institutions.

(a) nature, technology
(b) human, technology
(c) human, environment
(d) climate, soil

MCQs 2 Marks Questions

19. Consider the following statements about the Resource Planning in India.

I. The availability of resources is a necessary condition for the development of any region.

II. There are many regions in our country that are rich in resources but these are included in economically backward regions.

III. On the contrary, there are some regions which have a poor resource base, but they are economically developed.

Codes

(a) Only I (b) Both I and II
(c) Only II (d) All of these

20. Complete the flowchart.

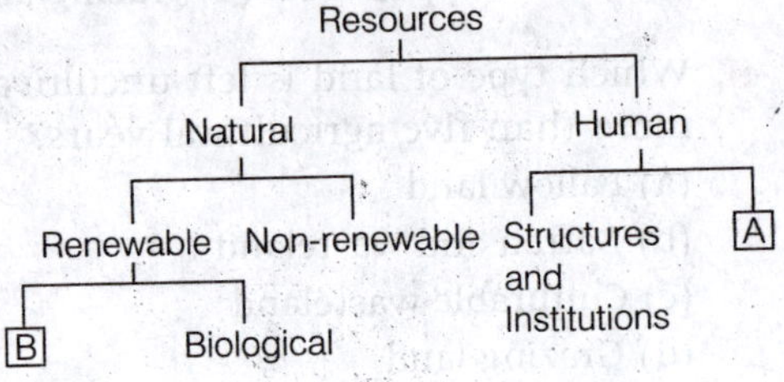

	A	B
(a)	Quantity and Quality	Continuous
(b)	Wildlife	Recyclable
(c)	Non-recyclable	Wildlife
(d)	Transport	Natural Vegetation

21. Match the following.

List I	List II
A. Laterite soil	1. High moisture retention
B. Black soil	2. Intensively cultivated
C. Alluvial soil	3. Source of salt
D. Arid soil	4. Problem of leaching

Codes

	A	B	C	D
(a)	1	2	3	4
(b)	4	3	2	1
(c)	3	2	4	1
(d)	4	1	2	3

22. Read the following statements and select which ones are true (T) and which ones are false.

I. The history of colonisation reveals that rich resources in colonies were the main attractions for the foreign invaders.

II. At the international level, the Club of Rome advocated resource conservation for the first time in a more systematic way in 1968.

III. Mining sites are abandoned after excavation work is complete leaving deep scars and traces of over-burdening.

IV. The laterite soil develops under tropical and sub-tropical climate with alternate wet and dry season.

Codes

	I	II	III	IV		I	II	III	IV
(a)	T	T	F	F	(b)	F	T	F	T
(c)	T	F	T	T	(d)	T	T	T	T

23. There are two statements marked as Assertion (A) and Reason (R). Mark your answer as per the codes given below.

Assertion (A) The lower horizon of the arid soil is occupied by kankar.

Reason (R) There is increasing calcium content downwards in arid soil.

Codes

(a) Both A and R are true and R is the correct explanation of A

(b) Both A and R are true, but R is not the correct explanation of A

(c) A is true , but R is false

(d) A is false, but R is true

24. Read the following passage and answer the following question.

Ploughing along the contour lines can decelerate the flow of water down the slopes. This is called contour ploughing. Large fields can be divided into strips. Strips of grass are left to grow between the crops. This breaks up the force of the wind. This method is known as strip cropping.

The given methods are used for which of the following purposes?

(a) To save trees

(b) For land degradation

(c) Water logging

(d) Soil conservation

25. Identify the types of soils marked as A and B on the given map of India.

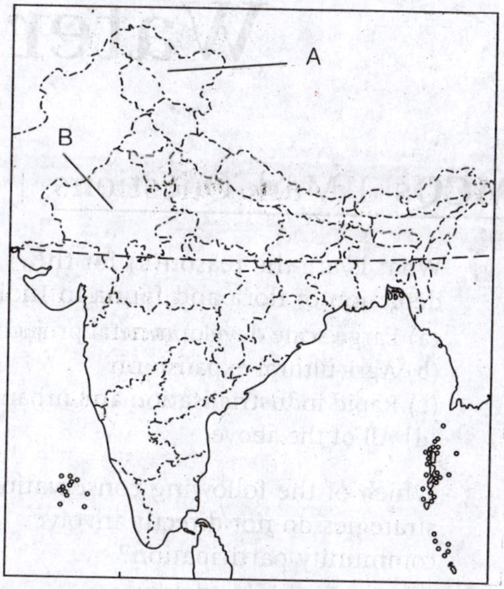

	A	B
(a)	Alluvial soil	Red soil
(b)	Forest soil	Arid soil
(c)	Arid soil	Forest soil
(d)	Laterite soil	Arid soil

Darken your choice with HB Pencil

1.	ⓐ ⓑ ⓒ ⓓ	6.	ⓐ ⓑ ⓒ ⓓ	11.	ⓐ ⓑ ⓒ ⓓ	16.	ⓐ ⓑ ⓒ ⓓ	21.	ⓐ ⓑ ⓒ ⓓ
2.	ⓐ ⓑ ⓒ ⓓ	7.	ⓐ ⓑ ⓒ ⓓ	12.	ⓐ ⓑ ⓒ ⓓ	17.	ⓐ ⓑ ⓒ ⓓ	22.	ⓐ ⓑ ⓒ ⓓ
3.	ⓐ ⓑ ⓒ ⓓ	8.	ⓐ ⓑ ⓒ ⓓ	13.	ⓐ ⓑ ⓒ ⓓ	18.	ⓐ ⓑ ⓒ ⓓ	23.	ⓐ ⓑ ⓒ ⓓ
4.	ⓐ ⓑ ⓒ ⓓ	9.	ⓐ ⓑ ⓒ ⓓ	14.	ⓐ ⓑ ⓒ ⓓ	19.	ⓐ ⓑ ⓒ ⓓ	24.	ⓐ ⓑ ⓒ ⓓ
5.	ⓐ ⓑ ⓒ ⓓ	10.	ⓐ ⓑ ⓒ ⓓ	15.	ⓐ ⓑ ⓒ ⓓ	20.	ⓐ ⓑ ⓒ ⓓ	25.	ⓐ ⓑ ⓒ ⓓ

Chapter 07

Forest, Wildlife and Water Resources

MCQs 1 Mark Questions

1. What is/are the reason(s) for the depletion of flora and fauna in India?
   (a) Large scale developmental projects
   (b) Agricultural expansion
   (c) Rapid industrialisation and urbanisation
   (d) All of the above

2. Which of the following conservation strategies do not directly involve community participation?
   (a) Beej Bachao Andolan
   (b) Joint Forest Management
   (c) Demarcation of Wildlife Sanctuaries
   (d) Chipko Movement

3. Where does mithun, an endemic cattle is found?
   (a) Assam
   (b) Andaman and Nicobar
   (c) Arunachal Pradesh
   (d) Kerala

4. .... is the site dedicated to preservation of one-horned rhinoceros.
   (a) Kaziranga National Park
   (b) Bandhavgarh National Park
   (c) Buxa Wildlife Reserve
   (d) All of the above

5. Which of the following animals of India are critical on the threatened list?
   (a) Cheetah (b) Pink-headed duck
   (c) Mountain quail (d) All of these

6. What factor(s) is/are responsible for depletion of forest and wildlife?
   (a) Mining
   (b) Grazing
   (c) Agricultural expansion
   (d) All of the above

7. Which among the following is not a vulnerable species in India?
   (a) Asiatic elephant (b) Blue sheep
   (c) Indian rhinoceros (d) Gangetic dolphin

8. When did the Indian Wildlife (Protection) Act introduced?
   (a) 1980 (b) 1982
   (c) 1997 (d) 1972

9. In which among the following National Parks, the 'Project Tiger' (1973) was first introduced?
   (a) Jim Corbett (Uttarakhand)
   (b) Kaziranga (Assam)
   (c) Kanha National Park (Madhya Pradesh)
   (d) Simiplipal National Park (Odisha)

10. Which of the following movements show that adequate levels of diversified crop production without the use of synthetic chemicals are possible and economically viable?
(a) Beej Bachao Andolan and Navdanya
(b) Chipko Movement and Navdanya
(c) Joint Forest Management and Chipko Movement
(d) Chipko Movement and Water Management

11. The Asiatic Cheetah was declared extinct in India long back in ....
(a) 1972
(b) 1973
(c) 1952
(d) 1992

12. The species that are not found after searches of known or likely areas where they may occur are known as ....
(a) normal species
(b) vulnerable species
(c) extinct species
(d) rare species

13. Which of the following remote backward villages in Mysore, Karnataka installed household rooftop rainwater harvesting system?
(a) Vanasthalipuram
(b) Chilkunda
(c) Kallahalli
(d) Gendathur

14. Complete the given analogy.
Joint Forest Management : Odisha : : Beej Bachao Andolan : ?
(a) Chamoli
(b) Rudraprayag
(c) Tehri
(d) Uttarkashi

15. Which among the following trees are worshipped by Mundas and Santhal tribes of Chota Nagpur Plateau?
(a) Mahua
(b) Kadamba
(c) Tamarind
(d) Both (a) and (b)

16. Name the region of India which experience low rainfall and is drought prone.
(a) Bihar
(b) Gujarat
(c) Telangana
(d) Rajasthan

17. Who among the following proclaimed the dam as the 'Temple of Modern India'?
(a) Lal Bahadur Shashtri
(b) Mahatma Gandhi
(c) Motilal Nehru
(d) Jawaharlal Nehru

18. Identify the dam which is located on Narmada river and is famous due to prolonged agitation.
(a) Rana Pratap Sagar Dam
(b) Kayna Dam
(c) Sardar Sarovar Dam
(d) Mettur Dam

19. Where does rooftop rainwater harvesting is chiefly practiced?
(a) Tamil Nadu
(b) Eastern Rajasthan
(c) Western Rajasthan
(d) Eastern Kerala

20. Why water is considered as a renewable resource?
(a) 3/4th of the Earth is covered with water.
(b) It is available everywhere on the Earth.
(c) Large amount of fresh water is stored as groundwater.
(d) Existence of a hydrological cycle on the Earth.

21. In the given image, the techniques of rain water harvesting is given. Identify the correct statement(s) about rooftop rainwater harvesting from the following options.

(a) Rooftop rainwater harvesting was commonly practiced to store drinking water.
(b) The jhaud is a part of the well developed rooftop rainwater harvesting system.
(c) Rooftop rainwater harvesting is mostly practiced in urban areas.
(d) All of the above

MCQs 2 Marks Questions

22. Read the case study given below and answer the following question.

The Himalayan Yew *(Taxus Wallachiana)* is a medicinal plant found in various parts of Himachal Pradesh and Arunachal Pradesh. It is a medicinal plant which is an anti- cancer treatment drug. However, the species is under great threat due to over-exploitation.

What can be done to save this plant species?

(a) The government should impose heavy fines on people who are indulged in the indiscriminate cutting of this plant species.
(b) Community participation is necessary in order to save this species.
(c) Both (a) and (b)
(d) None of the above

23. There are two statements marked as Assertion (A) and Reason (R). Mark your answer as per the codes given below.

Assertion (A) Humans are themselves responsible for depletion of their forests and wildlife.

Reason (R) Humans transformed nature for obtaining reserves directly and indirectly from the forests.

Codes

(a) Both A and R are true and R is the correct explanation of A
(b) Both A and R are true, but R is not the correct explanation of A
(c) A is true, but R is false
(d) A is false, but R is true

24. Fill in the blanks by choosing the correct options.

......(I)...... are species which are in danger of extinction. The survival of such species is difficult if the ......(II)...... factors that have led to a decline in their population continue to operate.

	I	II
(a)	Endangered species	negative
(b)	Normal species	positive
(c)	Rare species	negative
(d)	Endangered species	positive

25. Match the following.

List I (Multipurpose Projects)	List II (River)
A. Salal Project	1. Mahanadi river
B. Rana Pratap Sagar	2. Krishna river
C. Nagarjuna Sagar	3. Chambal river
D. Hirakud	4. Chenab river

Codes

	A	B	C	D
(a)	1	2	3	4
(b)	4	3	2	1
(c)	2	4	1	3
(d)	2	1	3	4

26. Consider the following statements.

I. A dam is a barrier across flowing water that obstructs, directs or retards the flow, often creating a reservoir, lake or impoundment.

II. Most dams have a section called a spillway or weir over which or through which it is intended that water will flow either intermittently or continuously.

III. Dams in India are used for internal navigation purpose, irrigation purpose and fish breeding.

Codes

(a) I and II (b) II and III
(c) I and III (d) All of these

27. Read the following statements and select which ones are true (T) and which ones are false (F).

I. India's rivers, especially the smaller ones, have all turned into toxic streams.

II. Reserved forests are owned by the government and all the human activities are not allowed in these forests.

III. By announcing the Jal Jeevan Mission (JJM), government of India has accorded highest priority to improve the quality of life and enhance ease of living of people, especially those living in rural areas.

IV. Reserved forests constitute about more than half of the total forest land in India.

Codes

	I	II	III	IV
(a)	T	T	F	T
(b)	T	T	T	T
(c)	F	F	T	T
(d)	T	F	T	F

28. Identify the dams marked as A and B on the given map of India.

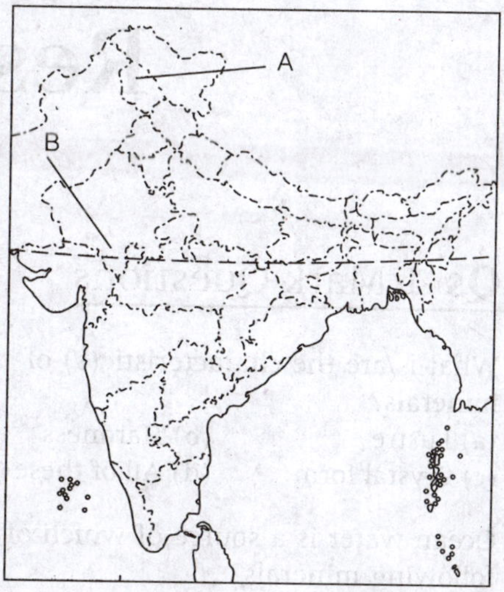

	A	B
(a)	Salal	Rana Pratap Sagar
(b)	Sardar Sarovar	Tungabhadra
(c)	Bhakra Nangal	Tehri
(d)	Tungabhadra	Sardar Sarovar

Darken your choice with HB Pencil

1. ⓐ ⓑ ⓒ ⓓ	6. ⓐ ⓑ ⓒ ⓓ	11. ⓐ ⓑ ⓒ ⓓ	16. ⓐ ⓑ ⓒ ⓓ	21. ⓐ ⓑ ⓒ ⓓ	26. ⓐ ⓑ ⓒ ⓓ
2. ⓐ ⓑ ⓒ ⓓ	7. ⓐ ⓑ ⓒ ⓓ	12. ⓐ ⓑ ⓒ ⓓ	17. ⓐ ⓑ ⓒ ⓓ	22. ⓐ ⓑ ⓒ ⓓ	27. ⓐ ⓑ ⓒ ⓓ
3. ⓐ ⓑ ⓒ ⓓ	8. ⓐ ⓑ ⓒ ⓓ	13. ⓐ ⓑ ⓒ ⓓ	18. ⓐ ⓑ ⓒ ⓓ	23. ⓐ ⓑ ⓒ ⓓ	28. ⓐ ⓑ ⓒ ⓓ
4. ⓐ ⓑ ⓒ ⓓ	9. ⓐ ⓑ ⓒ ⓓ	14. ⓐ ⓑ ⓒ ⓓ	19. ⓐ ⓑ ⓒ ⓓ	24. ⓐ ⓑ ⓒ ⓓ	
5. ⓐ ⓑ ⓒ ⓓ	10. ⓐ ⓑ ⓒ ⓓ	15. ⓐ ⓑ ⓒ ⓓ	20. ⓐ ⓑ ⓒ ⓓ	25. ⓐ ⓑ ⓒ ⓓ	

Chapter 08

Minerals and Energy Resources

MCQs 1 Mark Questions

1. What is/are the characteristic(s) of minerals?
(a) Lustre (b) Hardness
(c) Crystal form (d) All of these

2. Ocean water is a source of which of the following minerals?
(a) Bromine (b) Magnesium
(c) Common Salt (d) All of these

3. In which of the following states, the Badampahar mine in Mayurbhanj and Kendujhar districts is situated?
(a) Chhattisgarh (b) Karnataka
(c) Jharkhand (d) Odisha

4. Durg-Bastar-Chandrapur belt lies in Chhattisgarh and ....
(a) Odisha (b) Maharashtra
(c) Karnataka (d) West Bengal

5. Where is very high grade haematite iron ore found in the hills of Bastar district of Chhattisgarh?
(a) Mainpat (b) Ambikapur
(c) Gadiya Mountain (d) Bailadila

6. Name the mineral which is formed by decomposition of rocks, leaving a residual mass of weathered material.
(a) Coal (b) Gold
(c) Zinc (d) Bauxite

7. Koderma is located in Jharkhand state. It is the leading producer of which one of the following minerals?
(a) Copper (b) Bauxite
(c) Iron ore (d) Mica

8. What method(s) is/are useful for the conservation of minerals?
(a) Mineral resources should be used in planned and sustainable manner.
(b) Technologies should be developed to use lower grade ores at lower costs.
(c) Metals should be recycled.
(d) All of the above

9. Where are the large reserves of natural gas have been discovered in India?
(a) Krishna Godavari Basin
(b) Gulf of Mannar
(c) Arabian Sea
(d) Andaman and Nicobar Islands

10. What does the given picture signifies?

(a) Construction work in progress
(b) Trapping of nuclear energy
(c) Conservation of minerals
(d) Mining

11. Which of the following is the highest quality hard coal?

(a) Lignite (b) Bituminous
(c) Anthracite (d) Peat

12. Identify the correctly matched pair.

(a) Kalol Oil Fields – Gujarat
(b) Chandrapur Thermal Power Plant – Odisha
(c) Mayurbhanj Iron ore Mines – Uttar Pradesh
(d) Amarkantak Bauxite Mine – Jharkhand

13. Thermal electricity is generated with the use of ....

(a) coal (b) natural gas
(c) petroleum (d) All of these

14. Which of the following minerals is found in the Monazite sand?

(a) Thorium (b) Coal
(c) Oil (d) Uranium

15. Where is the largest wind farm cluster located in India?

(a) Tamil Nadu (b) Andhra Pradesh
(c) Karnataka (d) Kerala

16. Nagercoil wind farm, which is very famous for effective use of wind energy is located in which state of India?

(a) Rajasthan (b) Odisha
(c) Kerala (d) Tamil Nadu

17. What is/are important use(s) of biogas in India?

(a) As a fuel
(b) For lighting purpose
(c) As a manure in farming
(d) All of the above

18. Minerals are deposited and accumulated in the stratas of .... rocks.

(a) metamorphic (b) igneous
(c) sedimentary (d) None of these

19. In India, the Gulf of Khambhat, the Gulf of Kachchh and the Gangetic delta provide ideal condition for utilising which energy?

(a) Wind energy
(b) Non-conventional energy
(c) Tidal energy
(d) Solar energy

MCQs 2 Marks Questions

20. Complete the flowchart.

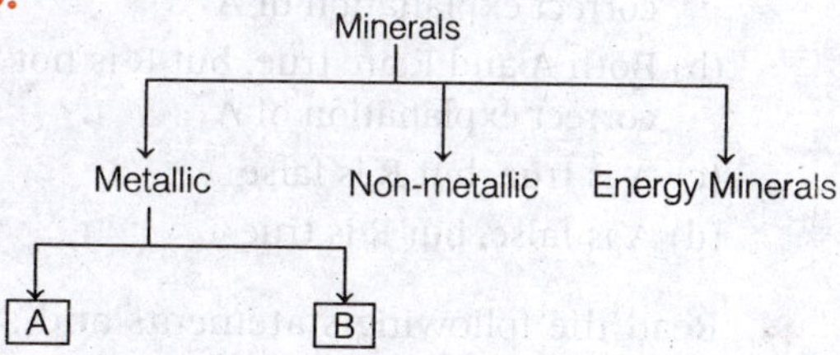

	A	B
(a)	Ferrous	Non-ferrous
(b)	Ferrous	Precious
(c)	Non-metallic	Ferrous
(d)	Precious	Basic

21. Arrange the following manganese producing states from highest to lowest production.

I. Andhra Pradesh II. Karnataka
III. Odisha IV. Madhya Pradesh

Codes

(a) II, I, III, IV (b) I, II, III, IV
(c) III, II, I, IV (d) IV, III, II, I

22. Match the following.

List I	List II
A. Ferrous minerals	1. Potash
B. Non-ferrous minerals	2. Nickel
C. Non-metallic minerals	3. Bauxite
D. Energy minerals	4. Uranium

Codes

	A	B	C	D		A	B	C	D
(a)	1	2	3	4	(b)	2	4	1	3
(c)	2	3	1	4	(d)	4	3	2	1

23. These are two statements marked as Assertion (A) and Reason (R). Mark your answer as per the codes given below.

Assertion (A) Anticlines and fault traps of tertiary rocks are associated with petroleum.

Reason (R) In anticline, folding or dome region, oil is trapped in the crest (top portion) of the upfold (stratified rocks).

Codes

(a) Both A and R are true and R is the correct explanation of A

(b) Both A and R are true, but R is not the correct explanation of A

(c) A is true, but R is false

(d) A is false, but R is true

24. Read the following statements and select which ones are true (T) and which ones are false (F).

I. Rajasthan has the largest share in limestone production in India.

II. Petroleum is also known as 'mineral oil'.

III. Flood gate dams are built across rivers so that water flows into inlet and gets trapped during high tides.

IV. Thermal energy is generated by burning fossil fuels that supply energy to drive turbines.

Codes

	I	II	III	IV
(a)	T	T	F	F
(b)	T	T	F	T
(c)	T	F	T	F
(d)	T	T	T	T

25. Identify the features marked as A and B on the given map of India with the help of following information.

A. Mica mine in Rajasthan

B. Iron ore mine in Karnataka

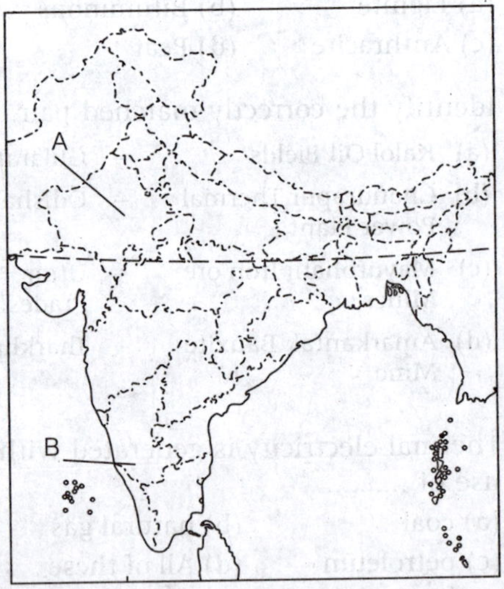

	A	B
(a)	Kudremukh	Bilaspur
(b)	Ajmer	Kudremukh
(c)	Aonia	Hazira
(d)	Amarkantak	Satpura

Darken your choice with HB Pencil

1.	(a) (b) (c) (d)	6.	(a) (b) (c) (d)	11.	(a) (b) (c) (d)	16.	(a) (b) (c) (d)	21.	(a) (b) (c) (d)
2.	(a) (b) (c) (d)	7.	(a) (b) (c) (d)	12.	(a) (b) (c) (d)	17.	(a) (b) (c) (d)	22.	(a) (b) (c) (d)
3.	(a) (b) (c) (d)	8.	(a) (b) (c) (d)	13.	(a) (b) (c) (d)	18.	(a) (b) (c) (d)	23.	(a) (b) (c) (d)
4.	(a) (b) (c) (d)	9.	(a) (b) (c) (d)	14.	(a) (b) (c) (d)	19.	(a) (b) (c) (d)	24.	(a) (b) (c) (d)
5.	(a) (b) (c) (d)	10.	(a) (b) (c) (d)	15.	(a) (b) (c) (d)	20.	(a) (b) (c) (d)	25.	(a) (b) (c) (d)

Chapter
09

Agriculture and Industries

MCQs 1 Mark Questions

1. Which of the following activities has been changed depending on the characteristics of physical environment, technological know-how and socio-cultural practice?

(a) Transport Network
(b) Industrial Activity
(c) Irrigation Pattern
(d) Cultivation

2. Identify the type of agriculture practice famous in North-Eastern states like Assam, Meghalaya, Mizoram and Nagaland.

(a) Subsistence farming
(b) Slash and burn farming
(c) Commercial farming
(d) Jhumming cultivation

3. In which of the following systems of agriculture a single crop is grown on a large area?

(a) Shifting agriculture
(b) Horticulture
(c) Intensive agriculture
(d) Plantation agriculture

4. Identify the type of agriculture shown in the given picture.

(a) Sugarcane plantation
(b) Cotton farming
(c) Coffee plantation
(d) Banana plantation

5. Main crops like paddy, maize, jowar, bajra, etc are grown during which of the following seasons?

(a) Summer (b) Spring
(c) Winter (d) Monsoon

6. Aus, Aman and Boro are types of .... crop.

(a) paddy (b) bajra
(c) jowar (d) maize

7. Identify the incorrectly matched pair.

(a) Sugarcane – Tropical as well as sub-tropical crop.

(b) Pulses – India's important source of protein.

(c) Cotton – It can be grown in sandy soil.

(d) Maize – Both food and fodder crop.

8. Name the crop that helps to fix nitrogen and restore soil fertility.

(a) Jowar (b) Millets
(c) Pulses (d) Sesamum

9. Where was coffee production introduced in India?

(a) Annamala hills
(b) Baba burdan hills
(c) Cardamom hills
(d) Palani hills

10. What is the reason for low production of jute?

(a) Jute mills are not technically advanced.
(b) Jute is loosing its market to synthetic fibres.
(c) Jute needs well drained fertile soils.
(d) Jute needs flood plains that should be renewed every year.

11. On which sources, most of the Indian farmers depend for irrigation?

(a) Tube wells (b) Monsoon
(c) Reservoirs (d) Rivers

12. .... is a scheme introduced by the Government of India to provide easy and cheap loans to small farmers.

(a) Kisan Empowerment Card
(b) Farmers Relief Fund
(c) Kisan Credit Card
(d) None of the above

13. Complete the given analogy.

Maize : Alluvial soil : : Jute : ?

(a) Sandy soil
(b) Laterite soil
(c) Red soil
(d) Well drained fertile soil in flood plains

14. Identify the feature(s) through which the ideal location of an industry is influenced.

(a) Decision to locate factory at site.
(b) Cost of obtaining raw materials at site.
(c) Cost of production a site.
(d) All of the above

15. Which of the following activities employ people in the manufacturing of primary materials into finished goods?

(a) Tertiary activities
(b) Primary activities
(c) Secondary activities
(d) Quaternary activities

16. .... is example of private sector industry.

(a) Bajaj Auto Limited
(b) Dabur Industries
(c) TISCO
(d) All of the above

17. Which among the following agencies markets steel for the public sector plants?

(a) TATA Steel (b) HAIL
(c) SAIL (d) MNCC

18. Identify the industry which uses limestone as a raw material.

(a) Cement
(b) Automobile
(c) Plastic
(d) Aluminium smelting

19. Which of the following industries uses bauxite as a raw material?
(a) Cement
(b) Steel
(c) Aluminium smelting
(d) Paper

20. Identify the incorrectly matched pair.
(a) Private Sector – SAIL
(b) Public Sector – BHEL
(c) Electric Power Generation – NTPC
(d) Joint Sector – OIL

21. Where is the cotton industry mainly located in India?
(a) Maharashtra (b) Gujarat
(c) Tamil Nadu (d) All of these

22. Why is primitive subsistence agriculture considered an old fashioned farming practice?
(a) There is no use of modern equipments in this farming.
(b) Farming is done with the help of primitive tools.
(c) This type of farming depends upon monsoon.
(d) All of the above

MCQs 2 Marks Questions

23. Arrange the following in chronological order.
I. Cotton mill set up at Mumbai.
II. Jute mill set up at Rishra.
III. First cement plant in Chennai.
IV. Formation of NTPC.

Codes
(a) III, II, IV, I (b) I, II, III, IV
(c) IV, II, I, III (d) III, IV, I, II

24. Consider the following statements about the requirements of the crop.
I. It requires tropical climate only.
II. It requires deep and fertile soil.
III. It requires abundant, cheap and skilled labour.

Which of the above statements is/are correct?
(a) I and II (b) II and III
(c) Only I (d) All of these

25. Match the following.

List I	List II
A. Wheat	1. Kharif
B. Rice	2. Zaid
C. Pulses	3. Rabi
D. Muskmelon	4. Both Rabi and Kharif

Codes

	A	B	C	D
(a)	2	4	3	1
(b)	1	2	3	4
(c)	3	1	4	2
(d)	1	4	2	3

26. There are two statements marked as Assertion (A) and Reason (R). Mark your answer as per the codes given below.

Assertion (A) Change in cropping pattern from cereals to high value crops is beneficial for Indian economy.

Reason (R) High value crops will increase income and reduce environmental degradation simultaneously.

Codes
(a) Both A and R are true and R is the correct explanation of A
(b) Both A and R are true, but R is not the correct explanation of A
(c) A is true, but R is false
(d) A is false, but R is true

27. Consider the following statements about millets.

I. Millets can grow easily in varied conditions.

II. Bajra, wheat and ragi are rainfed crops.

III. Millets provide plenty of micro-nutrients.

Which of the following statements are correct?

(a) I and II (b) II and III

(c) I and III (d) All of these

28. Fill in the blanks with appropriate words.

The ......(I)...... agriculture is known as 'Milpa' in Mexico and Central America, 'Conuco' in Venzuela, ...(II)...... in Brazil, 'Masole' in Central Africa, 'Ladang' in Indonesia, 'Ray' in Vietnam.

	I	II
(a)	slash and burn	'Roca'
(b)	intensive	'Kuruwa'
(c)	extensive	'Conuco'
(d)	plantation	'Khil'

29. Read the following statements and select which ones are true (T) and which ones are false (F).

I. Rabi crops are sown in winter from October to December and harvested in summer from April to June.

II. Some of the important rabi crops are wheat, barley, peas, gram and mustard.

III. India is the largest producer of sponge iron.

Codes

	I	II	III		I	II	III
(a)	T	T	F	(b)	T	T	T
(c)	F	F	T	(d)	T	F	F

30. Identify the following features marked as A and B on the given map of India with the help of following information.

A. A woollen textile industry in Punjab.

B. A cotton textile industry in Tamil Nadu.

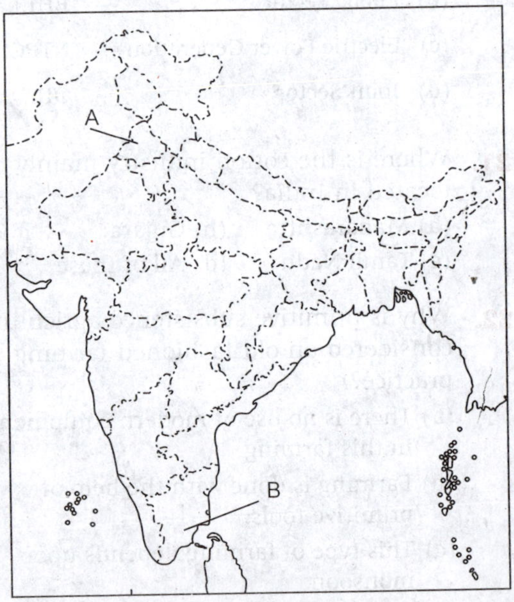

	A	B
(a)	Amritsar	Madurai
(b)	Bhatinda	Chennai
(c)	Patiala	Thanjavur
(d)	Jalandhar	Salem

Darken your choice with HB Pencil

1. ⓐ ⓑ ⓒ ⓓ	6. ⓐ ⓑ ⓒ ⓓ	11. ⓐ ⓑ ⓒ ⓓ	16. ⓐ ⓑ ⓒ ⓓ	21. ⓐ ⓑ ⓒ ⓓ	26. ⓐ ⓑ ⓒ ⓓ
2. ⓐ ⓑ ⓒ ⓓ	7. ⓐ ⓑ ⓒ ⓓ	12. ⓐ ⓑ ⓒ ⓓ	17. ⓐ ⓑ ⓒ ⓓ	22. ⓐ ⓑ ⓒ ⓓ	27. ⓐ ⓑ ⓒ ⓓ
3. ⓐ ⓑ ⓒ ⓓ	8. ⓐ ⓑ ⓒ ⓓ	13. ⓐ ⓑ ⓒ ⓓ	18. ⓐ ⓑ ⓒ ⓓ	23. ⓐ ⓑ ⓒ ⓓ	28. ⓐ ⓑ ⓒ ⓓ
4. ⓐ ⓑ ⓒ ⓓ	9. ⓐ ⓑ ⓒ ⓓ	14. ⓐ ⓑ ⓒ ⓓ	19. ⓐ ⓑ ⓒ ⓓ	24. ⓐ ⓑ ⓒ ⓓ	29. ⓐ ⓑ ⓒ ⓓ
5. ⓐ ⓑ ⓒ ⓓ	10. ⓐ ⓑ ⓒ ⓓ	15. ⓐ ⓑ ⓒ ⓓ	20. ⓐ ⓑ ⓒ ⓓ	25. ⓐ ⓑ ⓒ ⓓ	30. ⓐ ⓑ ⓒ ⓓ

Chapter 10

The Lifelines of National Economy

MCQs 1 Mark Questions

1. Name the corridor that links Srinagar and Kanyakumari.
   (a) North-East Corridor
   (b) South-West Corridor
   (c) North-South Corridor
   (d) East-West Corridor

2. Which of the following extreme locations are connected by the East-West Corridor?
   (a) Mumbai and Kolkata
   (b) Mumbai and Nagpur
   (c) Nagpur and Siliguri
   (d) Silchar and Porbandar

3. Choose the incorrect statement about National Highways.
   (a) National Highways link extreme parts of India.
   (b) National Highways No. 1 connects Delhi and Amritsar.
   (c) The historical Sher Shah Suri Marg is called National Highway No. 1.
   (d) National Highways are laid and maintained by the National Public Works Department.

4. ………… received special impetus under the Pradhan Mantri Gramin Sadak Yojana.
   (a) Border roads (b) State highways
   (c) Rural roads (d) District roads

5. Which of the following is the feature of Metalled roads ?
   (a) All weather roads
   (b) Unpaved roads
   (c) Dry season roads
   (d) Seasonal roads

6. What is the mode of transportation that reduces trans-shipment losses and delays?
   (a) Waterways (b) Roadways
   (c) Pipelines (d) Railways

7. Mumbai High and Bassein gas fields are linked with which important pipeline network of India?
   (a) Oil field in upper Assam to Kanpur pipeline network.
   (b) Salaya to Jalandhar pipeline network.
   (c) Hazira-Vijaipur-Jagdishpur (HVJ) pipeline network.
   (d) None of the above

8. Which one of the following states is not connected with the HVJ pipeline?
(a) Madhya Pradesh (b) Gujarat
(c) Uttar Pradesh (d) Maharashtra

9. Where is Jagdishpur gas pipeline located in India?
(a) Himachal Pradesh
(b) Madhya Pradesh
(c) Bihar (d) Uttar Pradesh

10. Why is it needed to develop Indian Railways?
(a) It is a cheap mode of transport.
(b) It is important for long distance travelling.
(c) It boosts the Indian economy by proving access to remove areas as well.
(d) All of the above

11. Name the first port which developed soon after independence to reduce the volume of trade on the Mumbai port.
(a) Karachi (b) Vizag
(c) Kandla (d) Kochi

12. Which of the following ports was developed as a subsidiary port in order to relieve growing pressure on the Kolkata port?
(a) Paradip port (b) Kochchi port
(c) Mangalore port (d) Haldia port

13. Identify the port which is the deepest portland-locked and well-protected port along the East Coast.
(a) Visakhapatnam (b) Paradip
(c) Chennai (d) Tuticorin

14. What is/are included in the commodities exported from India to other countries ?
(a) Gems and Jewellery
(b) Chemicals and related products
(c) Agriculture and allied products
(d) All of the above

15. .... promotes national integration and provides support to local handicrafts and cultural pursuits.
(a) Sports (b) Services
(c) Tourism (d) National Heritages

MCQs 2 Marks Questions

16. Arrange the following National Waterways as per their total length in India (in decreasing order).
I. National Waterway - 1
II. National Waterway - 3
III. National Waterway - 4
IV. National Waterway - 2

Codes
(a) I, II, III, IV (b) I, IV, II, III
(c) I, III, IV, II (d) I, III, II, IV

17. Consider the following statements about Golden Quadrilateral Super-Highways and identify which ones is/are true?
I. Golden Quadrilateral Super-Highways reduce the time and distance between mega cities of India.
II. East-West and North-South Corridors are part of this project.
III. Golden Quadrilateral Super-Highways link Delhi, Kolkata, Chennai, Mumbai and Delhi.

Codes
(a) Only I (b) II and III
(c) I and III (d) All of these

18. Read the following statements and select which ones are true (T) and which ones are false(F).
I. Mumbai is the biggest port in India.
II. Jawaharlal Nehru port is developed to ease off the decongestion in Mumbai port.
III. Mormugao port is the premier iron ore exporting port of the country.

IV. Tuticorin port is located in Andhra Pradesh.

Codes

	I	II	III	IV		I	II	III	IV
(a)	T	T	T	T	(b)	T	T	T	F
(c)	F	T	F	T	(d)	F	F	T	T

19. Match the following.

List I (Roads)	List II (Authority)
A. Golden Quadrilateral Super-Highways	1. Border Roads Organisation
B. State Highways	2. Zila Parishad
C. District Roads	3. State Public Works Department
D. Border Roads	4. National Highway Authority of India

Codes

	A	B	C	D
(a)	1	2	3	4
(b)	2	3	4	1
(c)	3	4	1	2
(d)	4	3	2	1

20. There are two statements marked as Assertion (A) and Reason (R). Mark your answer as per the codes given below.

Assertion (A) International trade is very essential and no country can survive without it.

Reason (R) Resources are space bound and no country is self-sufficient in every kind of resources.

Codes

(a) A and R are true and R is the correct explanation of A

(b) A and R are true, but R is not the correct explanation of A

(c) A is true, but R is false

(d) A is false, but R is true

21. Identify the features marked as A and B on the given map of India with the help of given information.

A. An International Airport in Punjab

B. An International Airport in Delhi

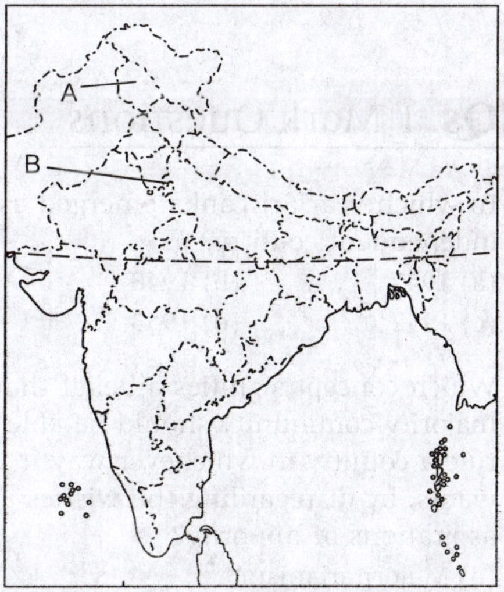

	A	B
(a)	Raja Sansi	Indira Gandhi International Airport
(b)	Patiala	Rajiv Gandhi International Airport
(c)	Bhatinda	Jawaharlal Nehru International Airport
(d)	Raja Sansi	Sonia Gandhi International Airport

Darken your choice with HB Pencil

1. ⓐ ⓑ ⓒ ⓓ	5. ⓐ ⓑ ⓒ ⓓ	9. ⓐ ⓑ ⓒ ⓓ	13. ⓐ ⓑ ⓒ ⓓ	17. ⓐ ⓑ ⓒ ⓓ	21. ⓐ ⓑ ⓒ ⓓ
2. ⓐ ⓑ ⓒ ⓓ	6. ⓐ ⓑ ⓒ ⓓ	10. ⓐ ⓑ ⓒ ⓓ	14. ⓐ ⓑ ⓒ ⓓ	18. ⓐ ⓑ ⓒ ⓓ	
3. ⓐ ⓑ ⓒ ⓓ	7. ⓐ ⓑ ⓒ ⓓ	11. ⓐ ⓑ ⓒ ⓓ	15. ⓐ ⓑ ⓒ ⓓ	19. ⓐ ⓑ ⓒ ⓓ	
4. ⓐ ⓑ ⓒ ⓓ	8. ⓐ ⓑ ⓒ ⓓ	12. ⓐ ⓑ ⓒ ⓓ	16. ⓐ ⓑ ⓒ ⓓ	20. ⓐ ⓑ ⓒ ⓓ	

Chapter 11

Power Sharing and Federalism

MCQs 1 Mark Questions

1. In which year Sri Lanka emerged as an independent country?
(a) 1947 (b) 1948
(c) 1952 (d) 1953

2. Which concept signifies a belief that the majority community should be able to rule a country in whichever way it wants, by disregarding the wishes and aspirations of minority?
(a) Majoritarianism
(b) Minoritarianism
(c) Federalism
(d) Despotism

3. What does the term LTTE stands for?
(a) Left Tribes of Tamil Estate
(b) Liberation Tigers of Tamil Eelam
(c) Liberation Tigers of Tamil Estate
(d) Liberation Tribes of Tamil Eelam

4. Identify the correct characteristic of Belgium from the options given below.
(a) Belgium is a small country in North America.
(b) Belgium has borders with France, Netherlands, Germany and Luxembourg.
(c) Spanish is majorly spoken in Belgium.
(d) In Brussels, the capital of Belgium, 80 per cent people speaks Dutch.

5. Where is the headquarters of European Union?
(a) Luxembourg
(b) Netherlands
(c) France
(d) Brussels

6. Which of the following is not an advantage of power sharing?
(a) It helps to reduce the possibility of conflicts between social groups.
(b) It helps to ensure the stability of the political order.
(c) It creates problem for the majority class of population.
(d) It increases the participation among citizen in formation of government.

7. .... is a system of government in which the power is divided between a central authority and various constituent units of the country.
(a) Parliament
(b) Democratic
(c) Federalism
(d) Unitarian

8. Identify the feature(s) of the unitary system.
(a) Centralisation of powers
(b) Flexibility of the Constitution
(c) Single government
(d) Both (a) and (c)

9. Identify the building given in the picture below.

(a) European Parliament Brussels
(b) Parliament of Sri Lanka
(c) French Parliament
(d) German Parliament (Bundestag)

10. Which of the following is not the form of power sharing?
(a) Vertical division of power.
(b) Horizontal division of power.
(c) Division of power between people.
(d) Division of power among social groups.

11. Name the country from the following options which is not an example of Holding Together Federations.
(a) Australia (b) Spain
(c) India (d) Belgium

12. Who among the following takes decision if there is a conflict in the laws made for the subjects in the Concurrent List?
(a) State Government
(b) Union Government
(c) President
(d) All of the above

13. Who can make laws on the issues [illegible] education, forest, trade unions, m[illegible] and adoption?
(a) State Government
(b) Union Government
(c) President of India
(d) Both (a) and (b)

14. .... has authority in administering the issues and affairs Union Territories of India.
(a) Union Government
(b) Chief Minister
(c) Both (a) and (b)
(d) Lt Governor

15. Which among the following states of India were not created on the basis of language but to recognise differences based on culture, ethnicity or geography?
(a) Jharkhand
(b) Uttarakhand
(c) Nagaland
(d) All of the above

16. ....the schedule of the Indian Constitution that deals with official language of India.
(a) Seventh (b) Eighth
(c) Fourth (d) Tenth

17. The use of English as official language was proposed to be stopped in which year?
(a) 1976 (b) 1965
(c) 1949 (d) 1974

18. Who has made it difficult for the central government to dismiss state government in an arbitrary manner?
(a) President
(b) Supreme Court
(c) District Court
(d) Constitution

19. Seats are reserved in the election bodies for specific castes group. Among which of the following castes such seats aren't reserved?

(a) Scheduled Castes
(b) Other Backward Castes
(c) Women
(d) Unreserved Castes

20. Complete the given analogy.

Power of National Government : Declare War : : Power of State Government : ?

(a) Provide public safety
(b) Establish foreign policy
(c) Interpret the Constitution
(d) Establish postal offices

21. A Gram Sabha should meet atleast .... in a year to approve annual budget and review the annual performance of Gram Sabha.

(a) once or twice (b) twice or thrice
(c) thrice (d) None of these

22. Which type of government is depicted in the image given below?

(a) Form of government in which political parties cooperate to form a government.
(b) A form of government whenever the country is ruled by a single political party.
(c) Federal government
(d) None of the above

MCQs 2 Marks Questions

23. Consider the following statements with reference to the relationship between central and state government and choose the correct option.

I. Our Constitution determines the extent of sharing of power between union and state government and it is the basic structure of the Constitution.
II. The Parliament can make changes to this power sharing arrangement.
III. In case of any dispute regarding the division of powers, the High Courts and Supreme Court make a decision.

Codes

(a) Only II (b) I and II
(c) II and III (d) I and III

24. Arrange in sequence according to the occurrence of the events.

I. States were created on the basis of language.
II. Rise of regional political parties leading to coalitions.
III. India's journey as a democracy begins.
IV. Central government agrees to continue the use of English.

Codes

(a) II,III,IV,I (b) III,I,IV,II
(c) IV,II,III,I (d) I,II,III,IV

25. Read the following statement and select which ones are true (T) and which ones are false (F).

I. Government of Sri Lanka formulated a policy of minorities for which it recognised Tamil as official language and favoured Tamil applicants in government jobs.
II. Belgium gained independence in 1830.
III. The USA and Switzerland have a federal system of government.

IV. At least two-third of all positions in local governments are reserved for women.

Codes

	I	II	III	IV
(a)	F	T	T	F
(b)	T	T	F	T
(c)	F	T	F	F
(d)	F	F	T	F

26. Match the following.

List I	List II
A. Sri Lanka gained independence	1. 1956
B. Sinhala became official language	2. 1948
C. Civil war of Sri Lanka ended	3. 2009

Codes

	A	B	C		A	B	C
(a)	1	3	2	(b)	2	1	3
(c)	3	1	2	(d)	1	2	3

27. Identify the organisation from the following information.

It was a Tamil militant organisation that was based on North-Eastern Sri Lanka fought to create an independent Tamil State called Tamil Eelam in the North-East of the island.

(a) ISIS (b) AQAP
(c) LTTE (d) ABM

28. There are two statements marked as Assertion (A) and Reason (R). Mark your answer as per the codes given below.

Assertion (A) Power is shared among different social groups in Belgium.

Reason (R) Community government in Belgium has the power regarding cultural educational and language related issue.

Codes

(a) Both A and R are true and R is the correct explanation of A
(b) Both A and R are true, but R is not the correct explanation of A
(c) A is true, but R is false
(d) A is false, but R is true

29. Identify the government body from the following information.

- He is responsible for conducting elections for Municipal Corporations in state and Conducting elections for Municipal Panchayats in state.
- He formulates model code of conduct to be implemented in elections for local bodies and also updates electoral rolls with new additions.

(a) Chief Election Commissioner
(b) Governor
(c) State Election Commissioner
(d) President

Darken your choice with HB Pencil

1. ⓐ ⓑ ⓒ ⓓ	6. ⓐ ⓑ ⓒ ⓓ	11. ⓐ ⓑ ⓒ ⓓ	16. ⓐ ⓑ ⓒ ⓓ	21. ⓐ ⓑ ⓒ ⓓ	26. ⓐ ⓑ ⓒ ⓓ
2. ⓐ ⓑ ⓒ ⓓ	7. ⓐ ⓑ ⓒ ⓓ	12. ⓐ ⓑ ⓒ ⓓ	17. ⓐ ⓑ ⓒ ⓓ	22. ⓐ ⓑ ⓒ ⓓ	27. ⓐ ⓑ ⓒ ⓓ
3. ⓐ ⓑ ⓒ ⓓ	8. ⓐ ⓑ ⓒ ⓓ	13. ⓐ ⓑ ⓒ ⓓ	18. ⓐ ⓑ ⓒ ⓓ	23. ⓐ ⓑ ⓒ ⓓ	28. ⓐ ⓑ ⓒ ⓓ
4. ⓐ ⓑ ⓒ ⓓ	9. ⓐ ⓑ ⓒ ⓓ	14. ⓐ ⓑ ⓒ ⓓ	19. ⓐ ⓑ ⓒ ⓓ	24. ⓐ ⓑ ⓒ ⓓ	29. ⓐ ⓑ ⓒ ⓓ
5. ⓐ ⓑ ⓒ ⓓ	10. ⓐ ⓑ ⓒ ⓓ	15. ⓐ ⓑ ⓒ ⓓ	20. ⓐ ⓑ ⓒ ⓓ	25. ⓐ ⓑ ⓒ ⓓ	

Chapter 12

Gender, Religion and Caste

MCQs 1 Mark Questions

1. .... is a form of pervasive hierarchical social division which is natural and unchangeable.
(a) Religion (b) Caste
(c) Gender (d) Race

2. What do you mean by 'gender division'?
(a) Division between rich and poor
(b) Division between males and females
(c) Division between urban and rural
(d) Division between educated and uneducated

3. The hierarchical unequal roles assigned to men and women by the society is known as ....
(a) sex-ratio
(b) economic differences
(c) gender division
(d) social differences

4. Which one of these doesn't refer to the 'Feminist Movement'?
(a) Giving voting right to the women.
(b) Improving educational and career opportunities for women.
(c) Training them in household jobs.
(d) Improving their political and legal status.

5. In which of the following countries the participation of women in public life is very high?
(a) Finland (b) Japan
(c) Estonia (d) Rome

6. A system that values men more and gives them power over women is called ....
(a) socialist (b) liberal
(c) patriarchy (d) matriarchy

7. What do you understand by stereotype?
(a) A fixed idea about a particular type of person or thing, which is often not true in reality.
(b) A strong unreasonable feeling of not liking or trusting somebody/something, especially when it is based on his/her/its race, religion or sex.
(c) Treating one person or group worse than others.
(d) Both (a) and (c)

8. Which of the following statements denote gender stereotypes?
(a) A man working as a chef in a renowned restaurant.
(b) A woman working as an IAS of the city.
(c) A young lady as housewife.
(d) A man running a boutique.

9. Identify the state which has a child sex-ratio below 900.
(a) Madhya Pradesh
(b) Bihar
(c) Kerala
(d) Haryana

10. In India, how much seats are reserved for women in local government?
(a) Fifty percent
(b) One-third
(c) One-fourth
(d) Two-third

11. Who believed that politics must be guided by ethics drawn from religion?
(a) GK Gokhale
(b) Swami Dayananda
(c) Swami Vivekananda
(d) Mahatma Gandhi

12. Communalism refers to a division based on ....
(a) religion
(b) caste
(c) gender
(d) socio-economic status

13. Which among the following is/are correct about the communalism?
(a) The followers of a particular religion just belong to one community.
(b) The fundamental interests of the followers of a particular religion are same.
(c) Any difference in the followers of particular religion is relevant for community life.
(d) All of the above

14. A person who doesn't discriminate others on the basis of religious belief is called ....
(a) feminist (b) secular
(c) liberal (d) conservative

15. Which country possess the feature of secularism except India?
(a) China (b) Saudi Arabia
(c) Vatican city (d) Iraq

16. What is incorrect about the nature of Communalism?
(a) The followers of a particular religion just belong to one community.
(b) The fundamental interests of the followers of particular religion are the same.
(c) Those people who follow different religion can follow the same ideologies.
(d) If the followers of different religion have some similarities, then these are superficial and immaterial. Their interests are bound to be different and it involves conflict.

17. Social structure of India is based upon the .... system.
(a) caste
(b) discrimination
(c) secularism
(d) equality

18. Which factor doesn't weaken the caste inequalities?
(a) Urbanisation
(b) Literacy rate
(c) Education
(d) Politics

MCQs 2 Marks Questions

19. The given poster affirming women's strength belongs to ....

(a) Uttar Pradesh (b) Bengal
(c) Kerala (d) Bihar

20. Consider the following statements about caste in politics and choose the correct option.

I. When parties choose their candidate or when governments are formed, political parties usually take care that representatives of different castes and tribes find a place in it.

II. Political parties and candidates in elections make appeals to caste sentiment to win the elections.

III. To gain support, political parties raise caste-based issues during elections to get political support, as 'one man one vote' system.

Codes

(a) Only I (b) Both I and II
(c) Only III (d) All of these

21. Read the following statements and select which ones are true (T) or which ones ore false (F).

I. The political expression of gender division and political mobilisation helped to improve women's role in public life.

II. The division based on religious differences are often expressed in the field of politics.

III. Politics also influence the caste system and caste identities by bringing them into the political arena.

IV. New kinds of caste group have come up in the political arena like 'backward' and 'forward' caste groups.

Codes

	I	II	III	IV		I	II	III	IV
(a)	T	T	F	F	(b)	F	F	T	F
(c)	T	T	T	T	(d)	F	T	T	F

22. There are two statements marked as Assertion (A) and Reason (R). Mark your answer as per the codes given below.

Assertion (A) There is no official religion for the Indian state for maintaining its democratic status.

Reason (R) Communalism is one of the major challenges to democracy in our country.

Codes

(a) Both A and R are true and R is the correct explanation of A
(b) Both A and R are true, but R is not the correct explanation of A
(c) A is true, but R is false
(d) A is false, but R is true

23. Match the following.

List I	List II
A. Urbanisation	1. Geographical and occupational movement of workers.
B. Occupational mobility	2. All genders having equal rights and opportunities.
C. Feminist	3. Body of law regulating family relationships, including marriage and divorce, the treatment of children, and related economic matters.
D. Family law	4. The process by which large numbers of people become permanently concentrated in relatively small areas.

Codes

	A	B	C	D
(a)	4	2	3	1
(b)	4	1	2	3
(c)	3	2	4	1
(d)	1	2	3	4

24. Identify the personality from the following information.

- He was an Indian social activist, thinker and anti-caste social reformer.
- His work extended to many fields, including eradication of untouchability and the caste system.

(a) Jyotiba Phule
(b) Jawaharlal Nehru
(c) Sardar Patel
(d) Rajendra Prasad

Darken your choice with HB Pencil

1. ⓐ ⓑ ⓒ ⓓ	5. ⓐ ⓑ ⓒ ⓓ	9. ⓐ ⓑ ⓒ ⓓ	13. ⓐ ⓑ ⓒ ⓓ	17. ⓐ ⓑ ⓒ ⓓ	21. ⓐ ⓑ ⓒ ⓓ
2. ⓐ ⓑ ⓒ ⓓ	6. ⓐ ⓑ ⓒ ⓓ	10. ⓐ ⓑ ⓒ ⓓ	14. ⓐ ⓑ ⓒ ⓓ	18. ⓐ ⓑ ⓒ ⓓ	22. ⓐ ⓑ ⓒ ⓓ
3. ⓐ ⓑ ⓒ ⓓ	7. ⓐ ⓑ ⓒ ⓓ	11. ⓐ ⓑ ⓒ ⓓ	15. ⓐ ⓑ ⓒ ⓓ	19. ⓐ ⓑ ⓒ ⓓ	23. ⓐ ⓑ ⓒ ⓓ
4. ⓐ ⓑ ⓒ ⓓ	8. ⓐ ⓑ ⓒ ⓓ	12. ⓐ ⓑ ⓒ ⓓ	16. ⓐ ⓑ ⓒ ⓓ	20. ⓐ ⓑ ⓒ ⓓ	24. ⓐ ⓑ ⓒ ⓓ

Chapter 13

Political Parties

MCQs 1 Mark Questions

1. .... is a group of people, who came together to contest elections and hold power in the government.
   (a) Political party
   (b) Pressure group
   (c) Parliament
   (d) Interest group

2. In a country like India, who choose candidates for contesting elections?
   (a) Election Commissioner
   (b) Party Leader
   (c) General Public
   (d) Party Members

3. A tendency to take a side and inability to take a balanced view on the issue is known as ....
   (a) partisanship
   (b) favouritism
   (c) defection
   (d) participation

4. What is/are necessary for modern democratic countries to exist?
   (a) Elections
   (b) Opposition party
   (c) Majority party
   (d) All of the above

5. Identify incorrect option about the feature of political party.
   (a) All political parties have some policies or programmes for the society with a view to promote collective good.
   (b) Political parties reflect fundamental political divisions in a society.
   (c) Political parties favour certain part of the society.
   (d) Political parties can implement their policies by being in the opposition.

6. The political party system of China is an example of ....
   (a) non-party system
   (b) multi-party system
   (c) one-party system
   (d) two-party system

7. In which of the following countries there is a two-party system?
   (a) UK (b) Malta
   (c) Lebanon (d) All of these

8. In India, there is a multi- party system with more than 750 parties registered by the ....
   (a) President
   (b) Election Commission
   (c) Prime Minister
   (d) High Court

9. Who among the following is the founder of Bahujan Samaj Party?
(a) Jyotiba Phule
(b) BR Ambedkar
(c) Kanshi Ram
(d) Sahu Maharaj

10. What is the guiding philosophy of the Bharatiya Janata Party?
(a) Integral humanism
(b) Bahujan Samaj
(c) Modernity
(d) Revolutionary democracy

11. Identify the incorrectly matched pair.
(a) Telugu Desam Party – State Party
(b) Bharatiya Janata Party – National Democratic Alliance
(c) Congress Party – Left Front
(d) None of the above

12. Which of the following is/are essential element(s) of a political party?
(a) Leaders
(b) Active Members
(c) Followers
(d) All of the above

13. Which among the following is not the function of political party?
(a) Form public opinion
(b) Recontest election
(c) Political education to the people
(d) Faith in violent methods

14. Name the party which believes in marxism and leninism.
(a) CPI-M (b) BJP
(c) AITC (d) INC

15. Identify a regional party from the following options.
(a) Dravida Munnetra Kazhagam (DMK)
(b) Bharatiya Janata Party (BJP)
(c) Bahujan Samaj Party (BSP)
(d) Communist Party of India (Marxist) CPI-M

16. How political parties can be reformed?
(a) By state funding of election.
(b) By reducing the role of muscle power.
(c) By reducing the role of money.
(d) All of the above

17. When did the All India Trinamool Congress (AITC) founded by Mamta Banerjee, recognised as National party?
(a) 2013
(b) 2016
(c) 2018
(d) 2017

18. Which of the following is/are challenge(s) to political parties?
(a) Dynastic succession
(b) Money and muscle power
(c) Lack of internal democracy within parties
(d) All of the above

19. Complete the given analogy.
All India Majlis-e-ittehadul Muslimeen : ? : : Shiromani Akali Dal : Punjab
(a) Orissa
(b) Telangana
(c) Kerala
(d) Maharashtra

20. What does the given cartoon, drawn during the presidency of George Bush in USA, suggests?

(a) Two-party system is ignored.
(b) Republican party faces many problems.
(c) Republican party is the only party.
(d) Corporate American dictates all major institutions of the country.

21. Complete the given analogy.
Indian National Congress (INC) : 1885 :: Bharatiya Janata Party (BJP) : ?
(a) 1964
(b) 1980
(c) 1998
(d) 1999

22. The given picture highlights a major issue which is mainly conducted by Indian women. Identify the issue.

(a) A religious procession
(b) A voting rally
(c) A rally for a political/economic issue
(d) A rally for Women Empowerment

MCQs 2 Marks Questions

23. Consider the following statements.
I. Parties shape public opinion by raising and highlighting an issue.
II. Opposition parties criticise government for their wrong policies and mobilise opposition to the government.
III. Political parties have no access to government machinery and welfare schemes.
IV. Political parties recruit leaders and make them ministers by giving proper training to them.

Which of the following statements are correct?
(a) I, II and III
(b) I and IV
(c) I, II and IV
(d) II, III and IV

24. Match the following.

	List I (Political Party)		List II (Symbol)
A.	Shiromani Akali Dal	1.	Balanaced Scale or weighing balance
B.	Samajwadi Party	2.	Bicycle
C.	AIADMK	3.	Two leaves
D.	All India Trinamool Congress	4.	Flower and grass

Codes

	A	B	C	D
(a)	4	3	1	2
(b)	2	3	4	1
(c)	3	4	1	2
(d)	1	2	3	4

25. Read the following statements and select which ones are true (T) and which ones are false (F).

I. Elephant is the election symbol of Bahujan Samaj Party (BSP).

II. Bharatiya Jana Sangh is the mother party of Bharatiya Janata Party (BJP).

III. National Congress Party was formed in 1990.

IV. The symbol of National People's Party is book.

Codes

	I	II	III	IV
(a)	T	T	F	F
(b)	T	T	F	T
(c)	T	T	T	T
(d)	F	F	F	T

26. There are two statements marked as Assertion (A) and Reason (R). Mark your answer as per the codes given below.

Assertion (A) Nationalist Congress Party was formed in 1999.

Reason (R) It is a major party in Maharashtra and demands for Gandhian secularism, democracy, social justice and federalism.

Codes

(a) Both A and R are true and R is the correct explanation of A

(b) Both A and R are true, but R is not the correct explanation of A

(c) A is true, but R is false

(d) A is false , but R is true

27. Fill in the blanks with appropriate words.

Berlusconi was the Prime Minister of ...... (I) .... He is also one of the top businessmen in the country. He is the leader of the ...... (II) ...... founded in 1993. His company owns TV channels, the most important publishing company, a foot ball club ...... (III) ...... and a bank.

	I	II	III
(a)	Japan	Democratic Republic	Bayern Munich
(b)	Italy	Forza Italia	AC Milan
(c)	Greece	Greek Solution	AC Milan
(d)	Bangladesh	Jatiya Party	Bayern Munich

Darken your choice with HB Pencil

1. ⓐ ⓑ ⓒ ⓓ	6. ⓐ ⓑ ⓒ ⓓ	11. ⓐ ⓑ ⓒ ⓓ	16. ⓐ ⓑ ⓒ ⓓ	21. ⓐ ⓑ ⓒ ⓓ	26. ⓐ ⓑ ⓒ ⓓ
2. ⓐ ⓑ ⓒ ⓓ	7. ⓐ ⓑ ⓒ ⓓ	12. ⓐ ⓑ ⓒ ⓓ	17. ⓐ ⓑ ⓒ ⓓ	22. ⓐ ⓑ ⓒ ⓓ	27. ⓐ ⓑ ⓒ ⓓ
3. ⓐ ⓑ ⓒ ⓓ	8. ⓐ ⓑ ⓒ ⓓ	13. ⓐ ⓑ ⓒ ⓓ	18. ⓐ ⓑ ⓒ ⓓ	23. ⓐ ⓑ ⓒ ⓓ	
4. ⓐ ⓑ ⓒ ⓓ	9. ⓐ ⓑ ⓒ ⓓ	14. ⓐ ⓑ ⓒ ⓓ	19. ⓐ ⓑ ⓒ ⓓ	24. ⓐ ⓑ ⓒ ⓓ	
5. ⓐ ⓑ ⓒ ⓓ	10. ⓐ ⓑ ⓒ ⓓ	15. ⓐ ⓑ ⓒ ⓓ	20. ⓐ ⓑ ⓒ ⓓ	25. ⓐ ⓑ ⓒ ⓓ	

Chapter 14

Development and Sectors of Indian Economy

MCQs 1 Mark Questions

1. Which of the following neighbouring countries of India has better performance in terms of human development than India?
(a) Pakistan
(b) Bangladesh
(c) Nepal
(d) Sri Lanka

2. Which currency is used to count the Per Capita Income of different countries in the world?
(a) Canadian Dollars
(b) Rupees
(c) Pounds
(d) US Dollars

3. On which of the following basis, the Human Development Report (HDR) published by UNDP compares the countries?
(a) Per-Capita Income
(b) Literacy Rate
(c) Both (a) and (b)
(d) National Income

4. Identify the non-material benefit(s) that improve(s) welfare of population.
(a) Freedom
(b) Equal treatment
(c) Security
(d) All of these

5. Name the international organisation that publishes Human Development Report.
(a) World Health Organisation
(b) United Nations Organisation
(c) World Bank
(d) United Nations Development Programme

6. The total number of children attending school as a percentage of total number of children in the same age group is called ....
(a) literacy rate
(b) level of education
(c) net attendance ratio
(d) gross enrollment ratio

7. What is the major reason for more dropout ratio in Bihar?
(a) Political instability
(b) Low IMR
(c) Poverty
(d) High income

8. Identify a good way to measure the quality of life in countries across the world.
(a) National Income
(b) Happiness Index
(c) Human Development Index
(d) Education

9. The .... helps in maintaining the nutritional levels of poor people by providing food at lower cost.
(a) ration shops
(b) public distribution system
(c) minimum support price
(d) None of the above

10. Groundwater is an example of which type of resource?
(a) Non-renewable resources
(b) Stock resources
(c) Renewable resources
(d) Private resources

11. Which of the following signifies the economic development by maintaining the natural resources for present and future use?
(a) Resource Planning
(b) Conservation of Resources
(c) Sustainable Development
(d) All of the above

12. On what basis, the sectors of economy are classified into public and private sectors?
(a) Number of workers employed in the enterprises
(b) Employment conditions
(c) The nature of economic activity
(d) Ownership of enterprises

13. Choose the activity which is not related to primary sector.
(a) Natural gas extraction
(b) Fishing
(c) Making of sugar
(d) Mining

14. Complete the given analogy.
Tertiary sector : ? : : Secondary sector : Construction work
(a) Trade (b) Textile
(c) Iron and Steel (d) All of these

15. GDP is the total value of .... during a particular year.
(a) all goods and services
(b) all intermediate goods and services
(c) all intermediate and final goods and services
(d) all final goods and services

16. What are the goods that are used as raw materials for further production called?
(a) Material goods
(b) Intermediate goods
(c) Final goods
(d) Consumer goods

17. The task of collection of data on employment and unemployment is done by which of the following organisations?
(a) KPO (b) UNDP
(c) BPO (d) NSSO (NSO)

18. What is the type of unemployment in which more number of people work than actually needed ?
(a) Seasonal unemployment
(b) Underemployed
(c) Disguised unemployment
(d) Over employed

19. Identify the incorrectly matched pair.

(a) Tertiary sector – Owner of a play school

(b) Unorganised sector – Five people working in a local dhaba

(c) Public sector – Labour working under contractor

(d) Private sector – A company producing electric equipments

20. The person in the picture given below seems to be which of the following?

(a) Labourer – Organised sector
(b) Skilled craftsmen – Unorganised sector
(c) Daily wage earner – Unorganised sector
(d) Shopkeeper – Unorganised sector

MCQs 2 Marks Questions

21. Match the following.

List I	List II
A. Per-capita Income	1. Average Income
B. National Income	2. Proper nutrition
C. Body Mass Index	3. Total Income
D. Decent Standard of Living	4. Human Development Index

Codes

	A	B	C	D
(a)	4	1	3	2
(b)	1	4	3	2
(c)	3	1	4	2
(d)	1	3	2	4

22. What does we get by dividing the total income of country with its population? Choose the correct option.

I. Average Income
II. National Income
III. Per-capita Income
IV. Total Income

Codes

(a) Only III (b) I and III
(c) I and II (d) All of these

23. Read the following passage and answer the following question.

A big land owner has purchased farm machinery worth ₹ 10 Lakh to mechanise his farms. 20 small labourers and their families working in his farms are dissatisfied with this decision.

Analyse the information to choose the suitable option from the given options.

(a) India has low HDI ranking.
(b) Income is inadequate measure of development.
(c) Development goals differ according to situations.
(d) Total income is more suitable for comparison.

24. There are two statements marked as Assertion (A) and Reason (R). Mark your answer as per the codes given below.

Assertion (A) Since the second half of the 20th century, scientists have been warning that the type and levels of development are not sustainable.

Reason (R) In the name of development, natural resources are exploited at a fast rate leading to their depletion.

Codes

(a) Both A and R are true and R is the correct explanation of A
(b) Both A and R are true, but R is not the correct explanation of A
(c) A is true, but R is false
(d) A is false , but R is true

25 Read the following statements and select which ones are true (T) and which ones are false (F).

I. India comes under the category low-middle income countries.

II. Non-renewable resources are those which will get exhausted after a few years of use.

III. Money in your pocket cannot buy all the goods and services that you may need to live well.

Codes

	I	II	III		I	II	III
(a)	F	F	T	(b)	F	T	F
(c)	T	T	T	(d)	T	F	T

26 Consider the following statements about GDP of a country.

I. Final value of bakery items.

II. Value of silk fabrics for sale in the market.

III. Purchase of sugarcane in the making of sugar.

Which of the above values should be added to find out GDP?

(a) I and II

(b) II and III

(c) Only III

(d) None of the above

27 Read the following passage and answer the following question.

A flower cultivator grows tulips, reaps a good crop and sells it to a trader. The trader exports the tulips and earns huge profit. This increased the GDP but the farmer is still not able to earn well. Why?

(a) Most of the profit is taken by the trader.

(b) The farmer is underemployed or disguised employed.

(c) Farmers, traders and exporters work in unorganised sector.

(d) All of the above

Darken your choice with HB Pencil

1.	ⓐ ⓑ ⓒ ⓓ	6.	ⓐ ⓑ ⓒ ⓓ	11.	ⓐ ⓑ ⓒ ⓓ	16.	ⓐ ⓑ ⓒ ⓓ	21.	ⓐ ⓑ ⓒ ⓓ	26.	ⓐ ⓑ ⓒ ⓓ
2.	ⓐ ⓑ ⓒ ⓓ	7.	ⓐ ⓑ ⓒ ⓓ	12.	ⓐ ⓑ ⓒ ⓓ	17.	ⓐ ⓑ ⓒ ⓓ	22.	ⓐ ⓑ ⓒ ⓓ	27.	ⓐ ⓑ ⓒ ⓓ
3.	ⓐ ⓑ ⓒ ⓓ	8.	ⓐ ⓑ ⓒ ⓓ	13.	ⓐ ⓑ ⓒ ⓓ	18.	ⓐ ⓑ ⓒ ⓓ	23.	ⓐ ⓑ ⓒ ⓓ		
4.	ⓐ ⓑ ⓒ ⓓ	9.	ⓐ ⓑ ⓒ ⓓ	14.	ⓐ ⓑ ⓒ ⓓ	19.	ⓐ ⓑ ⓒ ⓓ	24.	ⓐ ⓑ ⓒ ⓓ		
5.	ⓐ ⓑ ⓒ ⓓ	10.	ⓐ ⓑ ⓒ ⓓ	15.	ⓐ ⓑ ⓒ ⓓ	20.	ⓐ ⓑ ⓒ ⓓ	25.	ⓐ ⓑ ⓒ ⓓ		

Chapter 15

Money and Credit

MCQs 1 Mark Questions

1. A weaver weaving clothes, wants to exchange clothes for rice. Luckily, he meets a farmer who has rice and is willing to exchange it for the clothes. What is this situation known as?
   (a) Barter system
   (b) Exchange of goods
   (c) Incidence of wants
   (d) Double coincidence of wants

2. Money plays many important functions. What is the most important function of money?
   (a) Used in Monetary transactions
   (b) Medium of exchange
   (c) Used in banking transactions
   (d) Payment of loans

3. Raghav has surplus money so, he opens a bank account and deposits in it. Whenever he needs money, he can go to his bank and withdraw from there. This kind of deposit with the banks is known as ....
   (a) Term deposit
   (b) Fixed deposit
   (c) Surplus deposit
   (d) Demand deposit

4. A person can withdraw money by issuing a cheque. What is a cheque?
   (a) Paper especially valid to withdraw money only from account holder's account.
   (b) Paper for withdrawing money only from accounts of others.
   (c) Paper for depositing money.
   (d) Paper instructing the bank to pay a specific amount.

5. Which of the following are included in the modern forms of money?
   (a) Paper currency and Gold and Silver coins
   (b) Cheque
   (c) Currency notes and coins
   (d) Debit card and Credit card

6. What is the most important function of banks?
   (a) Open as many bank accounts as possible.
   (b) Give loans to government.
   (c) Accept deposits and extend loans.
   (d) Give loans to businesses.

7. Which of the following is not included in the terms of credit in a bank loan?
   (a) The time period of the loan
   (b) The rate of interest
   (c) The lender's land
   (d) The borrower's land

8. Which of the following options best describes the given picture?

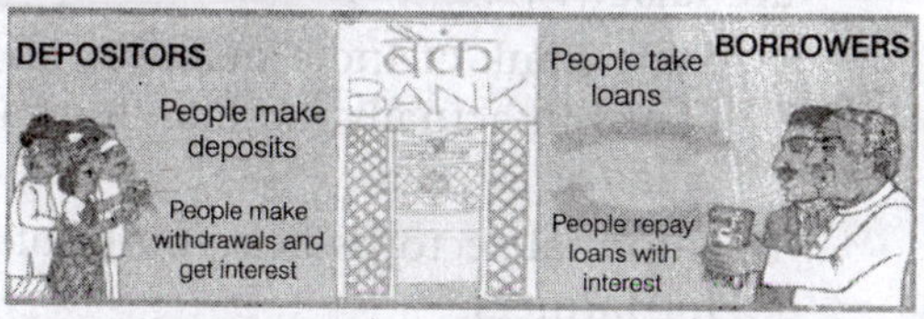

(a) Banks link depositors to borrowers.
(b) Banks are very important for the economy.
(c) Banks are useful in keeping surplus cash.
(d) Banks are mediator between depositors and borrowers.

9. Formal sources of credit do not include ....
(a) employers
(b) collateral
(c) banks
(d) cooperatives

10. Identify the statement which is not a feature of informal source of credit.
(a) Terms of informal source of credit are very flexible.
(b) Traders, employers, friends, relatives, etc provide informal source of credit.
(c) Informal source of credit is supervised by the Reserve Bank of India.
(d) Rate of interest is not fixed.

11. Banks give out loans and charge .... on the loan amount from the borrower.
(a) interest
(b) money
(c) collateral
(d) documents

12. Which among the following lenders gives loans without collateral?
(a) Private Agencies
(b) Banks
(c) Cooperatives
(d) Moneylenders

13. An important feature of Self Help Groups (SHGs) is that the members of such groups pool in their resources which together act as ....
(a) moneylenders
(b) employers
(c) collateral
(d) lenders

14. What does the percentages shown in the picture below represents?

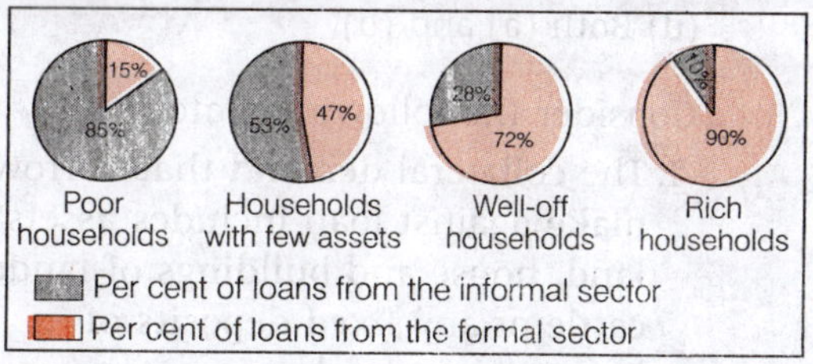

(a) Rich and poor households
(b) Credit given by formal and informal sector
(c) Informal and formal sector
(d) Loans pending with formal and informal sectors

15. Who supervised the credit activities of informal lenders?
(a) State government
(b) Reserve Bank of India
(c) Cooperatives
(d) None of the above

16. Complete the given analogy :
Formal source of credit : Banks ::
Informal source of credit : ?
(a) Moneylenders
(b) Traders
(c) SHGs
(d) All of the above

MCQs 2 Marks Questions

17. What could be done to eliminate the situation of debt-trap?
(a) To increase government source of credit.
(b) To improve the collateral condition for needy people.
(c) To encourage moneylenders to keep collateral with them.
(d) Both (a) and (b)

18. Consider the following statements.
I. The collateral demand that borrowers make against loan includes assets like land, house and buildings of landers, cattle or any fixed deposits of borrowers in banks.
II. Cheap and affordable credit is crucial for country's development.
III. Government make decisions regarding savings and loan activites in Self Help Groups (SHGs).

Which of the above statements is/are incorrect?
(a) I and II
(b) Only III
(c) II and III
(d) None of the above

19. Read the following statements and select which ones are true (T) and which ones are false (F).
I. State Bank of India monitors all the banks in actually maintaining cash balance.
II. Informal sector is best source of credit for farmers.
III. A cheque is a paper instructing the bank to pay a specific amount from the person's account to the person in whose name the cheque has been issued.
IV. Collateral is a form of money for banks.

Codes

	I	II	III	IV		I	II	III	IV
(a)	T	T	T	F	(b)	T	F	T	F
(c)	F	T	T	F	(d)	F	F	T	T

20. There are two statements marked as Assertion (A) and Reason (R). Mark your answer as per the codes given below.

Assertion (A) Borrowers when borrow from informal sources, they fall into debt traps.

Reason (R) Formal sector institutions need to lend more to the borrowers in order to prevent them from falling into debt-traps.

Codes
(a) Both A and R are true and R is the correct explanation of A
(b) Both A and R are true, but R is not the correct explanation of A
(c) A is true, but R is false
(d) A is false, but R is true

21. Read the case study given below and answer the following question.

Sunita owns a small flower shop near a temple. She wants to expand her shop by keeping exotic flowers and flower bouquets.

To whom she should approach for a very short term credit?

(a) Moneylenders as they provide short term credit.

(b) Cooperatives as they do not require collateral.

(c) Banks as they charge low interest.

(d) All of the above

22. Arrange in proper sequence.

I. Interest rate of loan is 5 per cent per annum.

II. Bank agrees to keep cold storage receipt as collateral.

III. Terms of credit is signed by Shyam.

IV. Shyam applies for a credit.

Codes

(a) IV, I, II, III (b) II, I, III, IV

(c) I, IV, II, III (d) III, I, IV, II

23. Read the case study given below and answer the following question.

Mahinder works in a private company while Sachin works as a daily wage earner. Both want a credit of ₹ 30,000/- . The bank is more likely to give credit to whom?

(a) Neither Mahinder nor Sachin

(b) Both Mahinder and Sachin

(c) Mahinder as he has regular employment

(d) Sachin as he is more needy

Darken your choice with HB Pencil

1. ⓐ ⓑ ⓒ ⓓ	5. ⓐ ⓑ ⓒ ⓓ	9. ⓐ ⓑ ⓒ ⓓ	13. ⓐ ⓑ ⓒ ⓓ	17. ⓐ ⓑ ⓒ ⓓ	21. ⓐ ⓑ ⓒ ⓓ
2. ⓐ ⓑ ⓒ ⓓ	6. ⓐ ⓑ ⓒ ⓓ	10. ⓐ ⓑ ⓒ ⓓ	14. ⓐ ⓑ ⓒ ⓓ	18. ⓐ ⓑ ⓒ ⓓ	22. ⓐ ⓑ ⓒ ⓓ
3. ⓐ ⓑ ⓒ ⓓ	7. ⓐ ⓑ ⓒ ⓓ	11. ⓐ ⓑ ⓒ ⓓ	15. ⓐ ⓑ ⓒ ⓓ	19. ⓐ ⓑ ⓒ ⓓ	23. ⓐ ⓑ ⓒ ⓓ
4. ⓐ ⓑ ⓒ ⓓ	8. ⓐ ⓑ ⓒ ⓓ	12. ⓐ ⓑ ⓒ ⓓ	16. ⓐ ⓑ ⓒ ⓓ	20. ⓐ ⓑ ⓒ ⓓ	

Chapter 16

Globalisation and the Indian Economy

MCQs 1 Mark Questions

1. In earlier times what did the trade consisted of?
   (a) Raw materials
   (b) Food stuffs
   (c) Finished goods
   (d) All of the above

2. What is the meaning of Multi-national Company?
   (a) A company that owns production in more than one country.
   (b) A company that owns production in only one country.
   (c) A company that owns production in its own company.
   (d) None of the above

3. What is the main reason due to which Multi-national Companies set up their branches in other countries?
   (a) To generate income
   (b) To generate employment
   (c) For welfare motive
   (d) For cheap labour and resources

4. Globalisation is/are possible through which of the following?
   (a) Foreign trade
   (b) Foreign investment
   (c) Trade barriers
   (d) Both (a) and (b)

5. When an MNC opens its company in India then it can be termed as ....
   (a) international trade
   (b) migration
   (c) foreign trade
   (d) foreign investment

6. Complete the given analogy.
   Cargill Foods : ? : : Parakh Foods : Indian Company
   (a) A smaller Indian MNCs
   (b) A large Russian Company
   (c) A large American MNCs
   (d) A large French Company

7. Who among the following gets more number of choices through foreign trade?
   (a) Government (b) Buyers
   (c) Producers (d) Sellers

8. The situation in which producers of one country are able to sell their goods in other countries is known as ....
   (a) exchange of goods
   (b) international trade
   (c) globalisation
   (d) foreign trade

9. What is the main role of foreign trade?
   (a) To manufacture high value products.
   (b) To set up factories only.
   (c) Connecting the markets or integration of markets in different countries.
   (d) To organise councils of trade.

10. In the competition between Indian and Chinese toys in Indian markets, why China proved better?
    (a) Good shape
    (b) Trade relations
    (c) Low price and variety
    (d) High price and quality

11. Which of the following is a problem with MNCs in India?
    (a) They invest only in rural areas.
    (b) They invest only in developing countries.
    (c) They invest only in urban/develop/well off areas.
    (d) They invest only in high source regions.

12. Identify the feature(s) of foreign trade from the options given below.
    (a) It facilitate movement of goods and services between countries.
    (b) It facilitate movement of people, ideas and technology.
    (c) It gives opportunity to producers to sell their products beyond local/domestic markets.
    (d) All of the above

13. Why have the central and state governments in India want to attract foreign companies in India?
    (a) To increase the production of foreign companies.
    (b) To improve the condition of Indian market.
    (c) To encourage local traders.
    (d) To improve the economy of India.

14. Which of the following is an important factor causing globalisation in India?
    (a) More income
    (b) Urbanisation
    (c) Expansion of markets
    (d) Technological developments

15. What the Indian government can do to check the free flow of Chinese goods in the Indian markets ?
    (a) Complain to UNO
    (b) Ban trade with China
    (c) Impose tax on exports
    (d) Impose tax on imports

16. Why did the Indian government restricted foreign trade after independence ?
    (a) To know the international level of quality
    (b) To increase competition
    (c) To protect domestic producers
    (d) All of the above

17. Which of the following has/have helped to give a greater choice of goods in the market to consumers?
    (a) Multi-national Companies
    (b) Increased foreign trade
    (c) Increased foreign investment
    (d) All of the above

18. What is the name of the situation in which all the countries reap equally the benefits of foreign trades?
(a) Liberalisation
(b) Equal globalisation
(c) Internationalisation
(d) Fair globalisation

19. Globalisation has led to improvement in living conditions of ....
(a) all the people
(b) people in the developed countries
(c) workers in the developing countries
(d) None of the above

20. Which type of countries has/have benefitted most from globalisation?
(a) Rich countries
(b) Developed countries
(c) Developing countries
(d) All of the above

21. Which of the following is not a feature of WTO?
(a) WTO was started at the initiative of developing countries.
(b) The aim of the WTO is to liberalise the foreign trade.
(c) WTO establishes rules regarding international trade for all countries and sees that they are obeyed.
(d) None of the above

MCQs 2 Marks Questions

22. Consider the following statements.
I. The Indian government, after independence, had put barriers to foreign trade and foreign investment.
II. Governments can use trade barriers to increase or decrease (regulate) foreign trade and to decide what kinds of goods and how much of each, should come into the country.

Which of the above statements is/are correct?
(a) Only I
(b) Only II
(c) Both I and II
(d) None of the above

23. Read the case study given below and answer the following question.
35 years old Sushila has spent many years as a worker in garment export industry of Delhi. She was employed as a 'permanent worker' entitled to health insurance, provident fund, overtime at a double rate, Sushila's factory closed in the late 1990s. After searching for a job for six months, she finally got a job 30 km away from where she lives. Even after working in this factory for several years, she is a temporary worker and earns less than half of what she was earning earlier.
What is/are the difference(s) between two job conditions of Sushila?
(a) First job indicates unorganised sector and second job indicates organised sector.
(b) First job indicates organised sector and second job indicates unorganised sector.
(c) First job was not suitable for Sushila.
(d) All of the above

24. There are two statements marked as Assertion (A) and Reason (R). Mark your answer as per the codes given below.

Assertion (A) Large MNCs in the garment industry look for cheapest goods from India as Indian exporters provide very cheap raw materials.

Reason (R) Since cost of raw materials cannot be reduced, Indian exporters cut labour costs and reduce wages in order to cut down their production cost.

Codes

(a) Both A and R are true and R is the correct explanation of A

(b) Both A and R are true, but R is not the correct explanation of A

(c) A is true, but R is false

(d) A is false, but R is true

25. Read the following statements and select which ones are true (T) and which ones are false (F).

I. Quotas are a way of restriction on volume or quality of goods to be imported or exported.

II. Removing barriers or restrictions set earlier by the government on foreign trade is known as liberalisation.

III. The money that is spent to buy assert such as land, building, machines and other equipment is called investment.

Codes

	I	II	III		I	II	III
(a)	T	T	T	(b)	F	F	T
(c)	T	F	F	(d)	F	T	F

26. Consider the following statements.

I. Large MNCs in developed countries place order for production with small producers.

II. Large MNCs have tremendous power to determine price, quality, delivery and labour conditions for these distant producers.

III. The most common route for MNC investments is to buy the local companies.

Which of the above statements is/are correct?

(a) Only I (b) I and II

(c) II and III (d) All of these

Darken your choice with HB Pencil

1. ⓐ ⓑ ⓒ ⓓ	6. ⓐ ⓑ ⓒ ⓓ	11. ⓐ ⓑ ⓒ ⓓ	16. ⓐ ⓑ ⓒ ⓓ	21. ⓐ ⓑ ⓒ ⓓ	26. ⓐ ⓑ ⓒ ⓓ
2. ⓐ ⓑ ⓒ ⓓ	7. ⓐ ⓑ ⓒ ⓓ	12. ⓐ ⓑ ⓒ ⓓ	17. ⓐ ⓑ ⓒ ⓓ	22. ⓐ ⓑ ⓒ ⓓ	
3. ⓐ ⓑ ⓒ ⓓ	8. ⓐ ⓑ ⓒ ⓓ	13. ⓐ ⓑ ⓒ ⓓ	18. ⓐ ⓑ ⓒ ⓓ	23. ⓐ ⓑ ⓒ ⓓ	
4. ⓐ ⓑ ⓒ ⓓ	9. ⓐ ⓑ ⓒ ⓓ	14. ⓐ ⓑ ⓒ ⓓ	19. ⓐ ⓑ ⓒ ⓓ	24. ⓐ ⓑ ⓒ ⓓ	
5. ⓐ ⓑ ⓒ ⓓ	10. ⓐ ⓑ ⓒ ⓓ	15. ⓐ ⓑ ⓒ ⓓ	20. ⓐ ⓑ ⓒ ⓓ	25. ⓐ ⓑ ⓒ ⓓ	

Chapter 17

Consumer Rights

MCQs 1 Mark Questions

1. The other name of goods that is used interchangeably in Economics is termed as ....

(a) article (b) things
(c) material (d) commodity

2. What do you mean by the term retailers?

(a) Shopkeepers who sell goods and services to people in large quantities.
(b) Shopkeepers who sell goods and services to people in small quantities.
(c) Shopkeepers who sell goods and services to producers in small quantities.
(d) None of the above

3. Which of the following ways is/are used by traders to exploit people at the market place?

(a) Not giving complete information about the product.
(b) Traders charging more price than listed.
(c) Giving less quantity.
(d) All of the above

4. Identify the correct option through which large companies exploit people.

(a) Listening to consumer complaints
(b) Ensuring consumer protection
(c) Helping in consumer movement
(d) Giving false information through media

5. What is the name of the consumer grievances redressal cell that was formed by Government of India?

(a) Consumer Protection Council
(b) Consumer Forum Council
(c) COPRA
(d) Consumer Disputes Redressal Commission.

6. The Bureau of Indian Standards gives a mark of certification to products of the Indian industries for quality assurance. Identify the mark.

(a) Agmark
(b) ISO
(c) COPRA
(d) ISI mark

7. The Consumer Protection Act, ensures that every consumer in India should possess .... Consumer Rights.

(a) four (b) two
(c) ten (d) six

8. United Nation adopted guidelines for consumer protection through Consumer International of ....

(a) 1999
(b) 2000
(c) 1985
(d) 2005

9. Identify the incorrect option about COPRA.

(a) COPRA stands for Consumer Protection Amendment.

(b) COPRA was enacted in 1987 by Government of India.

(c) Under COPRA, three tier quasi - judicial machinery was set up at district, state and national levels.

(d) All of the above

10. Which of the following is not a provision of Right to Seek Redressal?

(a) The consumer can file a complaint before the appropriate consumer forum on his/her own only with lawyers.

(b) While seeking any redressal, the consumers have the right to be represented in Consumer Courts.

(c) Consumers have the Right to Seek Redressal against unfair trade practices and exploitation.

(d) None of the above

11. Identify the mark in the picture given below.

(a) Agmark (b) Hallmark

(c) Woolmark (d) ISI

12. ISI mark is/are used for which of the following products?

(a) LPG cylinders (b) Automotive tyres

(c) Wiring cables (d) All of these

13. The Consumer Movement in India has led to the formation of various organisations locally known as ....

(a) Local Courts

(b) Redressal Forums

(c) Consumer Forum or Consumer Protection Councils

(d) None of the above

14. What is the certification mark that is employed on agricultural products in India?

(a) Agromark

(b) Woolmark

(c) Agmark

(d) Hallmark

15. Complete the given analogy.

Hallmark : Gold and Silver : : +F : ?

(a) Metals

(b) Gadgets

(c) Staple food products

(d) Silk clothes

MCQs 2 Marks Questions

16. Match the following.

List I	List II
A. District Consumer Court	1. Right to Information
B. Availing details of ingredients in a product	2. Deals with consumer cases
C. Bureau of Indian Standards	3. Certification of edible oil and cereals
D. Agmark	4. Global level institution of consumer welfare organisations

Codes

	A	B	C	D
(a)	1	2	3	4
(b)	4	2	1	3
(c)	3	4	1	2
(d)	2	1	4	3

17. Read the following statements and select which ones are true (T) and which ones are false (F).

I. Consumer protection council has got no legal right and is a voluntary organisation.

II. A consumer has the right to get compensation depending on the degree of the damage.

III. The consumer movement can become more effective only when consumers are made aware of their rights and their role in getting justice.

Codes

	I	II	III
(a)	T	F	T
(b)	T	T	T
(c)	F	F	T
(d)	T	F	F

18. Read the case study given below and answer the following question.

A person bought a packet of biscuits whose advertisement he saw in television. The packet has price, batch number, manufacturing and expiry date but does not mention its ingredients. It is the violation of which of the following rights?

(a) Right to Choice
(b) Right to Seek Redressal
(c) Right to Information
(d) Right to Safety

19. There are two statements marked as Assertion (A) and Reason (R). Mark your answer as per the codes given below.

Assertion (A) The Consumer Protection Act was enacted by the Supreme Court of India.

Reason (R) Consumer Protection Act helps to protect consumers against exploitation by the producers, sellers and service providers.

Codes

(a) Both A and R are true and R is the correct explanation of A
(b) Both A and R are true, but R is not the correct explanation of A
(c) A is true, but R is false
(d) A is false, but R is true

20. Consider the following statements.

I. Consumer forums are the organisations working for the rights of consumers.

II. Consumer forums provide assistance and guide the consumers to file cases in Consumer courts.

Choose the correct statement(s) from the codes given below.

(a) Only I (b) Only II
(c) Both I and II (d) None of these

21. Read the case study given below and answer the following question.

Raj want to buy toothpaste, and the shop owner says that she can sell the toothpaste only if he buys a toothbrush. However, he is not interested in buying the brush.

In the given situations, which right of Raj has been violated by the shop owner?

(a) Right to Select
(b) Right to Seek Redressal
(c) Right to Choose
(d) Right to Consumer Education

Darken your choice with HB Pencil

1.	ⓐ ⓑ ⓒ ⓓ	5.	ⓐ ⓑ ⓒ ⓓ	9.	ⓐ ⓑ ⓒ ⓓ	13.	ⓐ ⓑ ⓒ ⓓ	17.	ⓐ ⓑ ⓒ ⓓ	21.	ⓐ ⓑ ⓒ ⓓ
2.	ⓐ ⓑ ⓒ ⓓ	6.	ⓐ ⓑ ⓒ ⓓ	10.	ⓐ ⓑ ⓒ ⓓ	14.	ⓐ ⓑ ⓒ ⓓ	18.	ⓐ ⓑ ⓒ ⓓ		
3.	ⓐ ⓑ ⓒ ⓓ	7.	ⓐ ⓑ ⓒ ⓓ	11.	ⓐ ⓑ ⓒ ⓓ	15.	ⓐ ⓑ ⓒ ⓓ	19.	ⓐ ⓑ ⓒ ⓓ		
4.	ⓐ ⓑ ⓒ ⓓ	8.	ⓐ ⓑ ⓒ ⓓ	12.	ⓐ ⓑ ⓒ ⓓ	16.	ⓐ ⓑ ⓒ ⓓ	20.	ⓐ ⓑ ⓒ ⓓ		

Practice Sets

1-3

Practice Set 01

Time : 60 Mins. Max. Marks : 60

General Instructions

1. This question paper contains 50 questions.
2. All questions are compulsory. There is no negative marking.
3. Q. No. 1 to 40 are of 1 mark each and Q. No. 41 to 50 are of 2 marks each.
4. Use HB pencil / Blue ball point pen to mark your choice of answer by darkening the circles on the OMR Sheet.

MCQs 1 Mark Questions

1. Choose the correct nationality of the artist Frederic Sorrieu who visualised in his painting 'A society made up of Democratic and Social Republic'.

(a) German (b) Swiss
(c) French (d) American

2. In Africa in the 1890s, a fast-spreading disease of .... had a terrifying impact on people's livelihoods and the local economy.

(a) rinderpest (b) smallpox
(c) measles (d) scurvy

3. What is/are the feature(s) of multi-purpose river projects?

(a) Bring water to those areas which suffer from water scarcity.
(b) Multi-purpose projects lead to large-scale displacements and loss of livelihood.
(c) Generate electricity for our industries and our homes.
(d) Both (b) and (c)

4. Identify the correct statement regarding the difficulty faced by workers in a factory in 19th century in Britain.

(a) Employers were looking for only skilled workers and they rejected inexperienced applicants.
(b) The number of jobs were less than the number of job seekers.
(c) Employers did not prefer migrants.
(d) Employers wanted educated workers.

5. .... is a very good example of foundations challenge to democracy where monarchy was replaced by democratic system.

(a) Bolivia
(b) Myanmar
(c) Nepal
(d) USA

6. Identify the low grade brown coal, which is/are soft with high moisture content.

(a) Lignite
(b) Bituminous
(c) Anthracite
(d) Both (b) and (c)

7. The large MNCs have tremendous power to determine the ....
   (a) price
   (b) quality
   (c) labour conditions for these distant producers
   (d) All of the above

8. What is/are the characteristics of organised sector?
   (a) Workers in the organised sector enjoy the security of employment.
   (b) Workers are expected to work only a fixed number of hours.
   (c) If workers work more, they have to be paid overtime by the employer.
   (d) All of the above

9. Which among the following is not a threat to Indian Democracy?
   (a) Low gender ratio
   (b) Equal wages ratio
   (c) Caste system
   (d) Communalism

10. What do these newspaper clippings have to say about efforts of decentralisation in India?

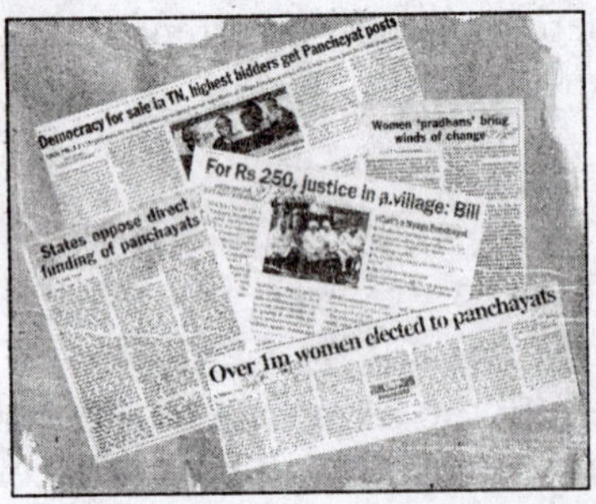

   (a) It shows that a huge number of women are elected in Panchayat.
   (b) Justice had been made easily accessible to villagers.
   (c) Panchayat are meant for the decentralisation of power.
   (d) All of the above

11. On which given subjects, both the union as well as the state governments make laws?
   (a) Currency
   (b) Defence
   (c) Trade Unions
   (d) Agriculture

12. Identify the incorrectly matched pair.
   (a) Gutenberg invented printing press – 1448
   (b) The first Malayalam book was printed – 1713
   (c) The Vernacular Press Act passed – 1878
   (d) Martin Luther wrote 'Ninety Five Theses' – 1517

13. Due to which reason, King Frederick William IV refused the crown of Germany presented by the Frankfurt Parliament?
   (a) He wanted to be crowned on his own terms.
   (b) He opposed the elected assembly.
   (c) As a true conservative he would accept it only from the German princes.
   (d) All of the above

14. Name the iron and steel plant which is located in Odisha.
   (a) Bhilai (b) Bhadravati
   (c) Salem (d) Rourkela

15. As per the Cenus 2011, which among the following states has the highest Infant Mortality Rate?
   (a) Kerala (b) Bihar
   (c) Maharashtra (d) Himachal Pradesh

16. What is the function of the District Consumer Court?
   (a) Produce the Right to Information about the goods
   (b) Certification of consumer products
   (c) Develop standards for goods and services
   (d) Dealing with consumer cases

17. What was the significance of the spinning wheel in the Flag created by Gandhi?
(a) It represented Swaraj.
(b) It represented the Gandhian ideal of self-help.
(c) It meant to boycott the foreign goods.
(d) None of the above

18. Which among the following is/are correct about the distribution of forest?
(a) Unclassed forests are forests and wastelands which are belonging to both government and private individuals and communities.
(b) Protected forests are the forests which are protected from any further depletion.
(c) Reserved forests are the most valuable forests as far as the conservation of forest and wildlife resources are concerned.
(d) All of the above

19. Sri Lanka is an island nation, just a few kilometres from the Southern coast of ....
(a) Goa (b) Kerala
(c) Tamil Nadu (d) Lakshadweep

20. Which of the following political parties opposed the forces of secessionism and communalism?
(a) Bahujan Samaj Party
(b) Bharatiya Janata Party
(c) Communist Party of India
(d) All India Trinamool Congress

21. What has been the major factor that stimulated the globalisation process?
(a) Availability of cheap labour in developing countries.
(b) Availability of unexploited resources in developing countries.
(c) Some countries are good in the landscape for natural resources.
(d) Rapid improvement in technology.

22. Overgrazing is the one of the main reasons for land degradation in ....
(a) Gujarat
(b) Rajasthan
(c) Madhya Pradesh
(d) All of the above

23. The given picture signifies which movement?

(a) Boycott of Foreign Cloth
(b) Civil Disobedience Movement
(c) Swadeshi Movement
(d) Khilafat Movement

24. When did the UK government and the Nationalists reach a peace treaty after which the latter suspended their armed struggle?
(a) 1995 (b) 1996
(c) 1997 (d) 1998

25. Complete the given analogy.
Khadins : Rajasthan : : Kuls or Guls : ?
(a) Manipur
(b) Himachal Pradesh
(c) Madhya Pradesh
(d) Punjab

26. Why modern currency is accepted as a medium of exchange?
(a) It is convenient.
(b) It has digital and manual system.
(c) It can be used in foreign exchange.
(d) It is authorised by the government of the country.

27. Under COPRA, a .... quasi-judicial machinery was setup for redressal of consumer disputes.
(a) three-tier
(b) one-tier
(c) two-tier
(d) four-tier

28. What does the concept sexual division of labour signify?
(a) Gender division on the basis of nature of work.
(b) Division between men and women.
(c) Caste is the basis of gender division.
(d) Both (a) and (b)

29. Who started the 'Bhoodan Movement', which is also known as Bloodless Movement in India?
(a) Mahatma Gandhi
(b) Jawaharlal Nehru
(c) Vinoba Bhave
(d) Sardar Patel

30. In which of the following options, power can be shared?
(a) Power is shared among different organs of government.
(b) Power can be shared among governments at different levels.
(c) Power may be shared among different social groups.
(d) All of the above

31. What was/were the impact(s) of the pace of industrial change?
(a) Jute and seal became the most dynamic industries in Britain.
(b) The modern machinery and industries could not easily displace traditional industries.
(c) Textile was a dynamic sector, but a large portion of the output was not produced within factories.
(d) Both (b) and (c)

32. What is/are the requirement(s) for the cultivation of wheat?
(a) It requires a cool growing season.
(b) It requires bright sunshine at the time of ripening.
(c) It requires 50 to 75 cm of annual rainfall.
(d) All of the above

33. The central government passed the law 'Right to Work' for how many districts of India?
(a) 300 (b) 520 (c) 625 (d) 460

34. Which of the following statements about Manuscripts is correct?
(a) It was easy to read from Manuscripts.
(b) It was easy to carry around the Manuscripts.
(c) Manuscripts were not fragile.
(d) None of the above

35. The .... covers activities in which natural products are changed into other forms through ways of manufacturing that we associate with industrial activity.
(a) secondary sector (b) tertiary sector
(c) primary sector (d) Both (b) and (c)

36. What is the most important function of banks?
(a) Accept deposits and extend loans.
(b) Open as many bank accounts as possible.
(c) Given loans to government.
(d) Give loans to businesses.

37. Why was/were the First World War also called the first modern industrial war?
(a) It saw the use of machine guns, tanks, aeroplanes, etc for the first time.
(b) Modern weapons were manufactured at large scale to modern industries.
(c) Many industries were destroyed in the war.
(d) Both (a) and (b)

38. Consider the following statements and choose the incorrect statement.

(a) In the Single Party system, only one party is allowed to control and run the government.

(b) In India, government is formed by various parties coming together in a coalition.

(c) USA and UK are examples of Multi-party System.

(d) None of the above

39. Complete the given analogy.
Black soil : Cotton :: Laterite soil : ?

(a) Coffee

(b) Wheat

(c) jute

(d) Bajra

40. In which year Asiatic Cheetah was declared as extinct in India?

(a) 1972

(b) 1952

(c) 2017

(d) 1982

MCQs 2 Marks Questions

41. Match the following.

List I (River Projects)	List II (Rivers)
A. Rana Pratap Sagar	1. Chambal
B. Nagarjuna Sagar	2. Krishna
C. Hirakud Project	3. Mahanadi
D. Sardar Sarovar Dam	4. Narmada

Codes

	A	B	C	D
(a)	1	2	3	4
(b)	4	3	2	1
(c)	2	1	4	3
(d)	3	4	1	2

Direction (Q. 42 & 43) Read the following passage and answer the following questions.

The English Press grew quite late in India even though the English East India Company began to import presses from the late 17th century. A weekly magazine named the Bengal Gazette was edited by James Augustus Hickey. By the end of the 18th century, a number of newspapers and journals appeared in print.

42. In the mid-16th century, the first printing press came to .... with Portuguese missionaries.

(a) Goa

(b) Tamil Nadu

(c) Odisha

(d) Kerala

43. In which year 'Bengal Gazette' a weekly English magazine was edited by James Augustus Hickey?

(a) 1880

(b) 1780

(c) 1905

(d) 1935

44. Consider the following statements about the legitimate government and choose the correct option.

I. In democracy, a legitimate government is a government where all the laws of the country are equally applicable to all citizens.

II. In this government, peoples are governed without fear or favour as well.

III. A legitimate government should be attentive to the needs and demands of the people.

Codes

(a) Only I (b) Only II

(c) Both I and II (d) All of these

45. Identify the port which is marked as A on the given map of India.

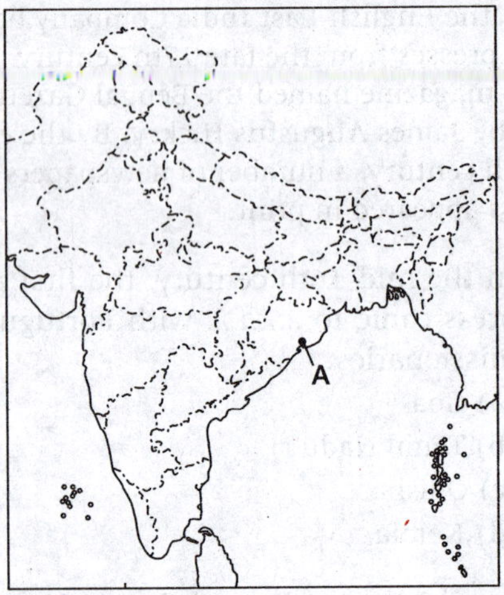

(a) Paradip port
(b) Kandla port
(c) Marmagao port
(d) Tuticorn port

46. Read the following statements and select which ones are true (T) and which ones are false (F).

I. Informal sector is the best source of credit for farmers.
II. State Bank of India monitors all the banks in actually maintaining cash balance.
III. Collateral is a form of money for banks.
IV. A deposit with a bank that can be withdrawn whenever the depositor wants to do, is known as a demand deposit.

Codes

	I	II	III	IV		I	II	III	IV
(a)	F	T	F	T	(b)	T	T	T	F
(c)	T	F	F	T	(d)	F	F	T	T

47. There are two statements marked as Assertion (A) and Reason (R). Mark your answer as per the codes given below.

Assertion (A) The Consumer Protection, Act was enacted in 1986 by the Indian Parliament.

Reason (R) Consumer Protection Act helps to protect consumers against exploitation by the producers, sellers and service providers.

Codes

(a) Both A and R are true and R is the correct explanation of A
(b) Both A and R are true, but R is not the correct explanation of A
(c) A is true, but R is false
(d) A is false, but R is true

48. Which among the following pairs is/are correctly matched?

I. National Waterway 1 – Allahabad to Haldia
II. National Waterways 2 – Sadiya to Dhubri
III. National Waterways 3 – West coast canal in Kerala to Udyogamandal
IV. National Waterways 4 – Varanasi to Hooghly

Codes

(a) Only I
(b) Both I and II
(c) Only III
(d) Only IV

49. Arrange in chronological order.

I. Quit India Movement
II. Dandi March
III. Jallianwala Bagh Massacre
IV. Poona Pact

Codes

(a) III, II, IV, I (b) I, III, II, IV
(c) II, III, IV, I (d) IV, I, III, II

50. Which of the following is/are correct about the features of democracy?

I. In democracy, the majority and minority opinions are not permanent.
II. In democracy, it is also necessary that rule by majority does not become rule by majority community in terms of religion or race or linguistic group.
III. Democracy remains democracy only as long as every citizen has a chance of being in majority at some point of time.

Codes

(a) Only I
(b) Only II
(c) Both I and II
(d) All of the above

Darken your choice with HB Pencil

1. ⓐ ⓑ ⓒ ⓓ	10. ⓐ ⓑ ⓒ ⓓ	19. ⓐ ⓑ ⓒ ⓓ	28. ⓐ ⓑ ⓒ ⓓ	37. ⓐ ⓑ ⓒ ⓓ	46. ⓐ ⓑ ⓒ ⓓ
2. ⓐ ⓑ ⓒ ⓓ	11. ⓐ ⓑ ⓒ ⓓ	20. ⓐ ⓑ ⓒ ⓓ	29. ⓐ ⓑ ⓒ ⓓ	38. ⓐ ⓑ ⓒ ⓓ	47. ⓐ ⓑ ⓒ ⓓ
3. ⓐ ⓑ ⓒ ⓓ	12. ⓐ ⓑ ⓒ ⓓ	21. ⓐ ⓑ ⓒ ⓓ	30. ⓐ ⓑ ⓒ ⓓ	39. ⓐ ⓑ ⓒ ⓓ	48. ⓐ ⓑ ⓒ ⓓ
4. ⓐ ⓑ ⓒ ⓓ	13. ⓐ ⓑ ⓒ ⓓ	22. ⓐ ⓑ ⓒ ⓓ	31. ⓐ ⓑ ⓒ ⓓ	40. ⓐ ⓑ ⓒ ⓓ	49. ⓐ ⓑ ⓒ ⓓ
5. ⓐ ⓑ ⓒ ⓓ	14. ⓐ ⓑ ⓒ ⓓ	23. ⓐ ⓑ ⓒ ⓓ	32. ⓐ ⓑ ⓒ ⓓ	41. ⓐ ⓑ ⓒ ⓓ	50. ⓐ ⓑ ⓒ ⓓ
6. ⓐ ⓑ ⓒ ⓓ	15. ⓐ ⓑ ⓒ ⓓ	24. ⓐ ⓑ ⓒ ⓓ	33. ⓐ ⓑ ⓒ ⓓ	42. ⓐ ⓑ ⓒ ⓓ	
7. ⓐ ⓑ ⓒ ⓓ	16. ⓐ ⓑ ⓒ ⓓ	25. ⓐ ⓑ ⓒ ⓓ	34. ⓐ ⓑ ⓒ ⓓ	43. ⓐ ⓑ ⓒ ⓓ	
8. ⓐ ⓑ ⓒ ⓓ	17. ⓐ ⓑ ⓒ ⓓ	26. ⓐ ⓑ ⓒ ⓓ	35. ⓐ ⓑ ⓒ ⓓ	44. ⓐ ⓑ ⓒ ⓓ	
9. ⓐ ⓑ ⓒ ⓓ	18. ⓐ ⓑ ⓒ ⓓ	27. ⓐ ⓑ ⓒ ⓓ	36. ⓐ ⓑ ⓒ ⓓ	45. ⓐ ⓑ ⓒ ⓓ	

Practice Set 02

Time : 60 Mins. Max. Marks : 60

General Instructions

1. This question paper contains 50 questions.
2. All questions are compulsory. There is no negative marking.
3. Q. No. 1 to 40 are of 1 mark each and Q. No. 41 to 50 are of 2 marks each.
4. Use HB pencil / Blue ball point pen to mark your choice of answer by darkening the circles on the OMR Sheet.

MCQs 1 Mark Questions

1. Giuseppe Mazzini founded the secret underground society named 'Young Europe' in ....

(a) Marseilles
(b) Berne
(c) Vienna
(d) Brussels

2. Why do we need the conservation and management of water?

(a) To meet the water demand effectively.
(b) To safeguard people from health hazards caused by drinking toxic water.
(c) To reduce over exploitation and mismanagement of water resources.
(d) All of the above

3. Which among the following Tiger Reserves is located in Rajasthan?

(a) Sariska Tiger Reserve
(b) Sunderbans Tiger Reserve
(c) Bandhavgarh Tiger Reserve
(d) Similipal Tiger Reserve

4. Which of the following statements is incorrect about political parties?

(a) Parties play a decisive role in making laws for a country.
(b) Parties didn't shape public opinion.
(c) Parties provide people with access to government machinery and welfare schemes.
(d) Parties have to be responsive to people's needs and demands.

5. Complete the given analogy.

Kharif crop : Jowar : : Rabi crop : ?

(a) Mustard (b) Cotton
(c) Cucumber (d) Groundnut

6. In the image given below, hungry children are digging for potatoes in a field that has already been harvested hoping to discover some left over. Which event does it resemble?

(a) Bengal Famine
(b) The Irish Potato Famine
(c) The France Potato Famine
(d) The USA Potato Famine

7. Johannes Gutenberg developed the first-known Printing Press in the 1430s, in Strasbourg that is located in which among the following countries?

(a) Great Britain (b) Germany

(c) USA (d) France

8. Which of the following is/are included in the terms of credit in a bank loan?

(a) The borrower's collateral

(b) The rate of interest

(c) Both (a) and (b)

(d) The lender's land

9. The location of an industry is influenced by the government policies and availability of ....

(a) raw material

(b) labour

(c) capital

(d) All of the above

10. Why a democratic government is much better than a non-democratic ?

(a) It has overwhelming support for the idea all over the world.

(b) It is a legitimate form of government.

(c) It allows us to correct our own mistakes.

(d) All of the above

11. The consumer movement in India has led to the formation of various organisations locally known as ....

(a) Local Courts

(b) Redressal Forums

(c) Consumer Forum or Consumer Protection Councils

(d) None of the above

12. Who among the following was/were the leader(s) of Hindustan Socialist Republican Army (HSRA)?

(a) Bhagat Singh

(b) Raj Guru

(c) Lala Lajpat Rai

(d) Subhash Chandra Bose

13. Irrigation has changed the cropping pattern of many regions with farmers shifting to water intensive and commercial crops. This has great ecological consequence for the soil. What is the consequence?

(a) Salinisation of the soil

(b) Contamination of soil

(c) Pollution of soil

(d) Excess of chemicals

14. Human Development Report published by UNDP compares countries on the basis of which of the following criterias?

(a) Health status (life expectancy)

(b) Per Capita Income

(c) Educational levels of the people(literacy rate)

(d) All of the above

15. The Consumer Protection Act, 1986 ensures some rights which every consumer in India should possess. There right include ....

(a) Right to Choice

(b) Right to Information

(c) Right to Rederessal

(d) All of the above

16. What did most of the conservatives believe in?

(a) Conservatives believed in monarchy.

(b) Conservatives believed in Church.

(c) Conservatives believed in social hierarchies.

(d) All of the above

17. What democracies ensure regarding the decision-making?

(a) Decisions are taken by the head of the country.
(b) The process of transparency.
(c) Decisions are taken by the Council of Ministers.
(d) Restricted popular participation in the decision-making.

18. .... from China introduced hand-printing technology into Japan around 768-770 AD.

(a) Buddhist Missionaries
(b) Christian Missionaries
(c) Scholars
(d) Traders

19. Which act empowers the people to find out what is happening in the government?

(a) Right to Information Act
(b) Right to Protection Act
(c) Right to Consumer Act
(d) Both (a) and (b)

20. What were the earliest form of objects used as money in India?

(a) Grains and cattle
(b) Coins
(c) Jewels
(d) Land

21. What is the integration between countries through foreign trade and foreign investments by Multi-national Corporations (MNCs) known as ?

(a) International trade
(b) Globalisation
(c) International investment
(d) World trade

22. Which among the following states of India has highest Child Sex Ratio?

(a) Chhattisgarh
(b) Gujarat
(c) Maharashtra
(d) Rajasthan

23. How did the East India Company setup a monopoly over the weaving industry in India?

(a) By openly fighting with the Portuguese and other traders.
(b) By dominating the weaver through force of action.
(c) By appointing the Gomasthas to get direct control over the weavers, providing loans and giving time limits.
(d) All of the above

24. What was the problem that the Europeans faced in Africa to carry out the work of plantations?

(a) Shortage of water
(b) Shortage of labour-willing to work for wages
(c) Lack of technology
(d) Rinderpest

25. Complete the given analogy.

Individual Resources : ? : : Community Owned Resources : Playgrounds

(a) Grazing grounds
(b) Public parks
(c) Picnic spots
(d) Pasture lands

26. Identify the language which is dominantly spoken in Belgium.

(a) Dutch
(b) French
(c) Spanish
(d) Italian

27. This party was founded in 1984 by Kanshi Ram to represent and secure power for the depressed classs. Identify the political party.

(a) Bahujan Samaj Party
(b) Samajwadi Party
(c) Communist Party of India
(d) Indian National Congress

28. Which among the following pair is not correctly matched ?

(a) Earliest factories start in England – 1730s
(b) First cotton mill setup in Bombay – 1854
(c) London underground railway start operation – 1863
(d) First jute mill owned by an Indian set up in Calcutta – 1934

29. The creation of .... was the first and a major test for democratic politics in India.

(a) states according to religion
(b) states according to culture
(c) linguistic states
(d) states according to topography

30. In December 1920, at the Congress Session in .... a compromise was worked out and the Non-Cooperation programme was adopted.

(a) Allahabad
(b) Bombay
(c) Nagpur
(d) Calcutta

31. Why did the Indian government restricted foreign trade after independence?

(a) To protect domestic producers
(b) To increase competition
(c) To know the international level of quality
(d) Both (b) and (c)

32. In Belgium, ... is a good example of power sharing among different social groups.

(a) community government
(b) district government
(c) central government
(d) state government

33. Which among the following is/are role(s) of public/government sector?

(a) Encouraging private sector to open industries and generate employment.
(b) This sector works for the welfare of the public and the overall development of the country.
(c) Dealing with problems of malnutrition, high Infant Mortality Rate, unsafe drinking water, lack of housing, food and nutrition.
(d) All of the above

34. In which part of Sri Lanka are the Sri Lankan Tamils concentrated?

(a) North and South
(b) North and East
(c) East and South
(d) West and North

35. It is the premier iron-ore exporting port in India. Identify the port.

(a) Marmagao (b) Kandla
(c) Paradip (d) Tuticorn

36. Which among the following states has the lowest Per Capita Income?

(a) Haryana (b) Bihar
(c) Kerala (d) Maharashtra

37. In which of the following regions, bauxite deposits are not found?

(a) Amarkantak Plateau
(b) Maikal Hills
(c) Plateau region of Bilaspur – Katni
(d) None of the above

38. Identify the sector of economy in the given picture.

(a) Primary sector
(b) Secondary sector
(c) Tertiary sector
(d) Both (a) and (c)

39. Soil erosion is the denundation of the upper layer of soil, identify the major reason(s) of it.
(a) Wind
(b) Water
(c) Overgrazing
(d) All of the above

40. What is/are the feature(s) of Primitive Subsistence Farming?
(a) Primitive Subsistence Farming is known as Jhumming in North-Eastern states.
(b) Land productivity is low in this primitive subsistence farming.
(c) This type of farming depends only upon monsoon.
(d) This type of farming is practiced in areas of high population pressure on land.

MCQs 2 Marks Questions

41. Match the following.

	List I		List II
A.	Coal	1.	Digboi
B.	Oil	2.	Maikal Hills
C.	Copper	3.	Raniganj
D.	Bauxite	4.	Khetri

Codes

	A	B	C	D
(a)	3	1	4	2
(b)	2	1	3	4
(c)	1	2	3	4
(d)	3	4	2	1

42. Identify the act from the following information.
- This Act had been hurriedly passed through the Imperial Legislative Council despite the united opposition of the Indian members.
- It gave the government enormous powers to repress political activities and allowed detention of political prisoners without trial for two years.

(a) Charter Act, 1853
(b) Rowlatt Act, 1919
(c) Regulating Act, 1773
(d) Government of India Act, 1935

43. Read the following statements and select which ones are true (T) and which ones are false (F).
I. The Reserve Bank of India supervises the functioning of formal sources of loans.
II. Cheap and affordable credit is crucial for the country's development.
III. The use of money spans a very large part of our everyday life.
IV. Credit (loan) refers to an agreement in which the lender supplies the borrower with money, goods or services in return for the promise of future payment.

Codes

	I	II	III	IV
(a)	T	T	T	T
(b)	T	T	T	F
(c)	T	F	T	F
(d)	F	F	T	T

44. Arrange the following in chronological order of their formation.

I. Maharashtra Navnirman Sena
II. Telangana Rashtra Samithi
III. Lok Janshakti Party
IV. Janata Dal

Codes

(a) IV, III, II, I
(b) I, II, III, IV
(c) II, IV, I, III
(d) III, I, IV, II

45. Identify the type of soil which is marked on the given map of India.

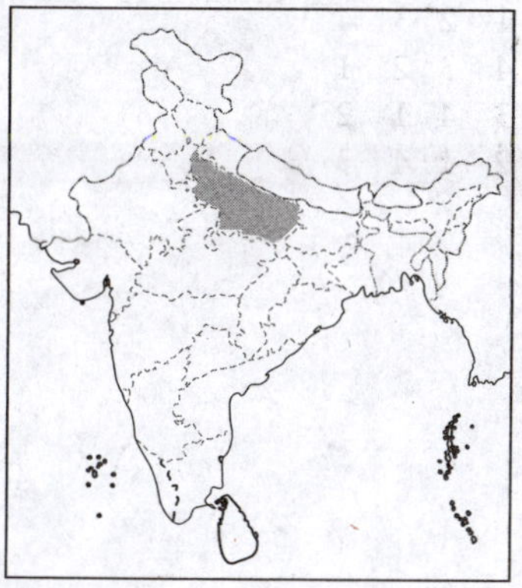

(a) Alluvial soil
(b) Laterite soil
(c) Black soil
(d) Desert soil

46. There are two statements marked as Assertion (A) and Reason (R). Mark your answer as per the codes given below.

Assertion (A) The secondary sector covers activities in which natural products are changed into other forms through ways of manufacturing that we associate with industrial activity.

Reason (R) Service sector also includes some essential services that may not directly help in the production of goods.

Codes

(a) Both A and R are true and R is the correct explanation of A
(b) Both A and R are true, but R is not the correct explanation of A
(c) A is true, but R is false
(d) A is false, but R is true

Direction (Q. 47 & 48) Read the following passage and answer the following questions.

After the defeat of Napoleon in 1815, European governments were driven by a spirit of conservatism. Conservatives, did not propose a return to the society of pre-revolutionary days. Rather, they realised from the changes initiated by Napoleon, that modernisation could in fact strengthen traditional institutions like the monarchy.

47. The term conservatism emphasise on which of the following?

(a) Importance of Tradition
(b) Established institution and customs
(c) Gradual development to quick change
(d) All of the above

48. Which among the following was not the representative of the European powers in 1815?

(a) Britain
(b) Russia
(c) Austria
(d) Germany

49. Consider the following statements and choose the correct option.

I. The air transport was nationalised in 1953.

II. India has one of the largest telecom networks in Asia.

III. India Radio Channel (Akashwani) broadcasts a variety of programmes in national, regional and local languages.

IV. Doordarshan, the National Television Channel is one of the largest terrestrial networks in the world.

Codes

(a) Only I

(b) Only IV

(c) Both I and III

(d) All of the above

50. Match the following.

List I (Regional Political Party)	**List II** (State)
A. Biju Janata Dal	1. Odisha
B. Rashtriya Janata Dal	2. Bihar
C. Indian National Lok Dal	3. Haryana
D. Samajwadi Party	4. Uttar Pradesh

Codes

	A	B	C	D
(a)	1	2	3	4
(b)	4	3	2	1
(c)	3	4	1	2
(d)	2	1	4	3

Darken your choice with HB Pencil

1.	ⓐ ⓑ ⓒ ⓓ	10.	ⓐ ⓑ ⓒ ⓓ	19.	ⓐ ⓑ ⓒ ⓓ	28.	ⓐ ⓑ ⓒ ⓓ	37.	ⓐ ⓑ ⓒ ⓓ	46.	ⓐ ⓑ ⓒ ⓓ
2.	ⓐ ⓑ ⓒ ⓓ	11.	ⓐ ⓑ ⓒ ⓓ	20.	ⓐ ⓑ ⓒ ⓓ	29.	ⓐ ⓑ ⓒ ⓓ	38.	ⓐ ⓑ ⓒ ⓓ	47.	ⓐ ⓑ ⓒ ⓓ
3.	ⓐ ⓑ ⓒ ⓓ	12.	ⓐ ⓑ ⓒ ⓓ	21.	ⓐ ⓑ ⓒ ⓓ	30.	ⓐ ⓑ ⓒ ⓓ	39.	ⓐ ⓑ ⓒ ⓓ	48.	ⓐ ⓑ ⓒ ⓓ
4.	ⓐ ⓑ ⓒ ⓓ	13.	ⓐ ⓑ ⓒ ⓓ	22.	ⓐ ⓑ ⓒ ⓓ	31.	ⓐ ⓑ ⓒ ⓓ	40.	ⓐ ⓑ ⓒ ⓓ	49.	ⓐ ⓑ ⓒ ⓓ
5.	ⓐ ⓑ ⓒ ⓓ	14.	ⓐ ⓑ ⓒ ⓓ	23.	ⓐ ⓑ ⓒ ⓓ	32.	ⓐ ⓑ ⓒ ⓓ	41.	ⓐ ⓑ ⓒ ⓓ	50.	ⓐ ⓑ ⓒ ⓓ
6.	ⓐ ⓑ ⓒ ⓓ	15.	ⓐ ⓑ ⓒ ⓓ	24.	ⓐ ⓑ ⓒ ⓓ	33.	ⓐ ⓑ ⓒ ⓓ	42.	ⓐ ⓑ ⓒ ⓓ		
7.	ⓐ ⓑ ⓒ ⓓ	16.	ⓐ ⓑ ⓒ ⓓ	25.	ⓐ ⓑ ⓒ ⓓ	34.	ⓐ ⓑ ⓒ ⓓ	43.	ⓐ ⓑ ⓒ ⓓ		
8.	ⓐ ⓑ ⓒ ⓓ	17.	ⓐ ⓑ ⓒ ⓓ	26.	ⓐ ⓑ ⓒ ⓓ	35.	ⓐ ⓑ ⓒ ⓓ	44.	ⓐ ⓑ ⓒ ⓓ		
9.	ⓐ ⓑ ⓒ ⓓ	18.	ⓐ ⓑ ⓒ ⓓ	27.	ⓐ ⓑ ⓒ ⓓ	36.	ⓐ ⓑ ⓒ ⓓ	45.	ⓐ ⓑ ⓒ ⓓ		

Practice Set 03

Time : 60 Mins. Max. Marks : 60

General Instructions

1. This question paper contains 50 questions.
2. All questions are compulsory. There is no negative marking.
3. Q. No. 1 to 40 are of 1 mark each and Q. No. 41 to 50 are of 2 marks each.
4. Use HB pencil / Blue ball point pen to mark your choice of answer by darkening the circles on the OMR Sheet.

MCQs 1 Mark Questions

1. Which area was the most serious source of nationalist tension in Europe after 1871?

(a) Southern Europe
(b) Mid Europe
(c) Balkan States
(d) Eastern States

2. When was the children's press, devoted to literature for children alone, set up in France?

(a) 1857 (b) 1517
(c) 1713 (d) 1868

3. What is/are the main reason(s) behind the occurence of thermal pollution?

(a) It is caused by the presence of high proportion of undesirable gases.
(b) It is caused by organic and inorganic waste.
(c) It occurs when hot water from factories and plants is drained into rivers and ponds before cooling.
(d) All of the above

4. For comparing the development of countries, their .... is considered to be one of the most important attributes.

(a) income
(b) population
(c) demographics
(d) Both (a) and (b)

5. Which of the following is/are the examples of the informal sector loans?

(a) Moneylenders (b) Traders
(c) Cooperatives (d) Both (a) and (b)

6. For consumer disputes the state level courts deal with cases involving claims between ₹ 20 lakh and ....

(a) ₹ 40 crores
(b) ₹ 20 crores
(c) ₹ 2 crores
(d) ₹ 1 crore

7. Which among the following is the correct chronological order?

(a) Napoleon invade Italy, Civil Code, Treaty of Vienna, Treaty of Constantinople
(b) Treaty of Vienna, Treaty of Constantinople, Napoleon invade Italy, Civil Code
(c) Treaty of Constantinople, Napoleon invade Italy, Treaty of Vienna, Civil Code
(d) Civil Code, Treaty of Constantinople, Napoleon invade Italy, Treaty of Vienna

8. Identify the incorrectly matched pair.

(a) Jallianwala Bagh Massacre	–	1913
(b) Oudh Kisan Sabha was set up	–	1920
(c) Demand of Purna Swaraj	–	1929
(d) Formation of Hindustan Socialist Republican Army (HSRA)	–	1928

9. Which type of farming has the use of higher doses of modern inputs, e.g. High Yielding Variety (HYV) seeds, chemical fertilisers, insecticides and pesticides?

(a) Primitive Subsistence Farming
(b) Plantation Farming
(c) Extensive Farming
(d) Commercial Farming

10. What was the impact on the handloom industry with the invention of the fly shuttle?

(a) It needed too much training.
(b) It increased productivity per worker, speeded up production and reduced labour demand.
(c) It reduced production.
(d) It was not very productive.

11. The largest wind farm cluster is located in Tamil Nadu from .... to ....

(a) Coimbatore, Madurai
(b) Nagercoil, Madurai
(c) Coonoor, Rameswaram
(d) Kanyakumari, Thanjavur

12. Complete the given analogy.
Indian National Congress : 1885 :
Bharatiya Janata Party : ?

(a) 1964
(b) 1980
(c) 1998
(d) 1999

13. On which of the following economic growth depends?

(a) Territory or area of the country
(b) Global scenario
(c) Size of the country's population
(d) Cooperation among the various nations

14. On the basis of ownership of enterprises, the sectors of economy are classified into how many sectors?

(a) Three (b) Two
(c) Four (d) One

15. Who mode the given picture of Bharat Mata in 1905?

(a) Rabindranath Tagore
(b) Abanindranath Tagore
(c) Raja Ravi Varma
(d) Raja Ram Mohan Roy

16. Which of the following is the world's oldest existing book printed with movable metal type?

(a) Diamond Sutra
(b) Pyrgi Gold Plates
(c) Jikji of Korea
(d) Gutenberg Bible

17. Identify the incorrect feature of the black soil.
(a) It is also known as cotton soil or regur soil.
(b) It is found in Deccan Trap Region.
(c) It is rich in phosphoric content.
(d) It is made up of lava-flows.

18. Who was/were the first Europeans to conquer America in mid-18th century?
(a) Russians
(b) The English and Portuguese
(c) Germans
(d) All of the above

19. What the Indian Government can do to check the free flow of Chinese goods in the Indian markets?
(a) Complain to UNO
(b) Impose tax on exports
(c) Ban trade with China
(d) Impose tax on imports

20. Why the Right to Information Act is a good example of a law that empowers the people?
(a) It helps to control corruption.
(b) It supplements the existing laws that banned corruption.
(c) It acts as a watchdog of democracy.
(d) All of the above

21. Which foods were introduced in Europe and Asia after Christopher Columbus discovered America?
(a) Potatoes, soya, groundnuts, maize, tomatoes, chillies, sweet potatoes
(b) Meat and potatoes
(c) Wheat, potatoes and rice
(d) Seafood, meat and wheat

22. What are the important things to do to prevent degradation of our natural ecosystems?
(a) Urbanisation
(b) Industrialisation
(c) Conserve and management of water resources to safeguard ourselves from health hazards.
(d) Modern agriculture

23. Which of the following factors not influenced the location of industry?
(a) Capital
(b) Labour
(c) Power and market
(d) Population density

24. When did the Civil War of Sri Lanka end?
(a) 2010
(b) 2009
(c) 2005
(d) 2011

25. More than half of the workers in the country are working in the primary sector, mainly in ....
(a) fishing
(b) mining
(c) agriculture
(d) business

26. What happened when the cotton industries developed in England in the 1850s onward?
(a) Manchester goods had to be sold in Britain, these goods were to be exported to India as well and import from India declined.
(b) English goods were not being sold in England due to quality problems.
(c) Demand for Indian textiles was more than Manchester goods.
(d) None of the above

27. In the capital city Brussels, 80 per cent people speak ...., while 20 per cent are .... speaking.
(a) French, Dutch
(b) Dutch, French
(c) French, German
(d) German, French

28. What is the advantage of a multi-party system?
(a) Multi-party system provides limited choice to voters.
(b) There is a chance of conflict in multi-party system.
(c) Multi-party system provides choice to the voters.
(d) In a multi-party system, regional parties get representation.

29. Which among the following is/are the factors of exploiting consumer?
(a) Selling sub-standard products
(b) Charging price more than listed
(c) Electronic goods lacking proper safety norms
(d) All of the above

30. Government purchases crop from farmers at which of the following prices?
(a) Minimum Support Price
(b) Maximum Support Price
(c) Both (a) and (b)
(d) Wholesale Price

31. What is the functioning of the system called, where power is shared among different organs of government, such as the legislature, executive and judiciary?
(a) Horizontal system
(b) System of checks and balances
(c) System of power sharing
(d) System of limited power

32. Who is the political head of Municipal Corporation?
(a) Zila Parishad
(b) Mayor
(c) Block Development Officer
(d) Member of Legislative Assembly

33. Land which is left without cultivation for one or less than one agricultural year is known as ....
(a) gross cropped area
(b) culturable waste land
(c) current fallow
(d) grazing land

34. Complete the given analogy.
Tuticorn Port : Tamil Nadu :: ? Gujarat
(a) Kandla (Deendayal) Port
(b) Marmagao Port
(c) Paradip Port
(d) Visakhapatnam Port

35. Identify the correct statement(s).
(a) Trade barrier is a restriction on the free International exchange of goods or services.
(b) Tax on imports is an example of trade barrier.
(c) Rapid improvement in technology has been one major factor that has stimulated the globalisation process.
(d) All of the above

36. On which of the following subjects can both the Union as well as the Sate Government make laws?
(a) Currency
(b) Defence
(c) Trade Unions
(d) Agriculture

37. In which article, the Constitution of India gives special status to some Indian states due to their peculiar social and historical circumstances?
(a) Article 371
(b) Article 271
(c) Article 172
(d) Article 152

38. Identify the correctly matched pair.
(a) Vulnerable Species – Black buck
(b) Endangered Species – Blue sheep
(c) Rare Species – Himalayan brown bear
(d) Extinct Species – Asiatic buffalo

39. In which article, the central and state governments in India have set up ...... to attract foreign companies to invest in India?

(a) Special Investment Zones
(b) Special Economic Zones
(c) Special Trade Zones
(d) Special Business Zones

40. In which year Muhammad Yunus, the founder of Grameen Bank of Bangladesh honoured with Nobel Prize ?

(a) 2006
(b) 2001
(c) 2013
(d) 2008

MCQs 2 Marks Questions

41. Match the following.

List I	List II
A. Broken chains	1. Being freed
B. Sword	2. Readiness to fight
C. Rays of the rising Sun	3. Beginning of the new era
D. Crown of oak leaves	4. Heroism

Codes

	A	B	C	D
(a)	1	2	3	4
(b)	4	3	2	1
(c)	2	1	4	3
(d)	3	4	1	2

42. There are two statements marked as Assertion (A) and Reason (R). Mark your answer as per the codes given below.

Assertion (A) Geologists define mineral as a 'homogenous, naturally occurring substance with a definable internal structure.

Reason (R) Minerals are found in varied forms in nature, ranging from the hardest diamond to the softest talc.

Codes

(a) Both A and R are true and R is the correct explanation of A
(b) Both A and R are true, but R is not the correct explanation of A
(c) A is true, but R is false
(d) A is false, but R is true

43. Arrange the following in chronological order.

I. Potato Famine in Ireland
II. The First World War
III. The Great Depression
IV. The Second World War

Codes

(a) IV, III, II, I
(b) I, II, III, IV
(c) II, IV, I, III
(d) III, I, IV, II

44. Consider the following statements.

I. Nature worship is an age old tribal belief based on the premise that all creations of nature have to be protected.
II. Endangered Species are species which are in danger of extinction.
III. The Indian Wildlife (Protection) Act was implemented in 1972, with various provisions for protecting habitats.

Identify the correct statement(s) from the codes given below.

(a) Only I
(b) I and II
(c) I and III
(d) All of the above

45. Identify the dam which is marked with A on the physical map of India.

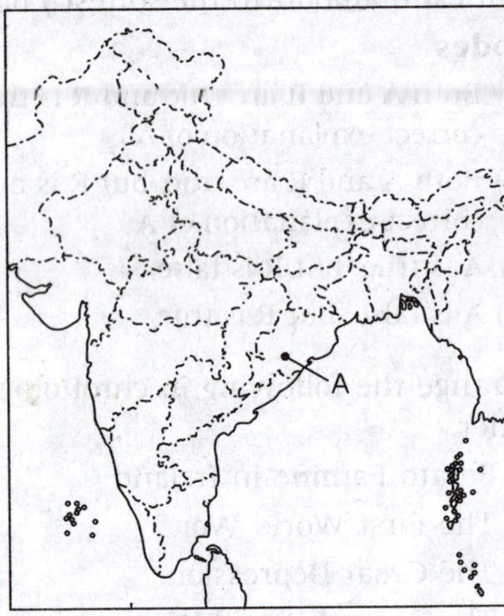

(a) Hirakud Dam
(b) Sardar Sarovar Dam
(c) Nagarjuna Sagar Dam
(d) Bhakra Nangal Dam

46. Match the following.

List I (Political Party)	List II (Symbol)
A. AIADMK	1. Bicycle
B. Samajwadi Pary	2. Flower and grass
C. All India Trinamool Congress	3. Balance scale or weighing balance
D. Shiromani Akali Dal	4. Two leaves

Codes

	A	B	C	D
(a)	1	2	3	4
(b)	4	1	2	3
(c)	2	1	4	3
(d)	3	1	2	4

Direction (Q. 47 & 48) Read the following passage and answer the following questions.

Under COPRA, a three-tier quasi-judicial machinery at the District, State and National levels was set up for redressal of consumer disputes. The enactment of COPRA has led to the setting up of separate Departments of Consumer Affairs in central and state governments. The posters that you have seen are one example through which government spread information about legal process which people can use. You might also be seeing such advertisements on television channels.

47. In which year, COPRA was enacted?

(a) 1986 (b) 2005
(c) 1982 (d) 1989

48. Identify the objective(s) of COPRA.

(a) To ensure better protection of interests of consumer.
(b) To protect consumer against unfair trade practice.
(c) Both (a) and (b)
(d) Neither (a) nor (b)

49. Identify the personality from the given information.

He organised the Dalits into the Depressed Class Association in 1930.

He demanded reserved seats in educational institutions and a separate electorate that would choose Dalit members for Legislative Council.

(a) Mahatma Gandhi (b) BR Ambedkar
(c) Shaukat Ali (d) Muhammad Ali

50. Read the following statements and select which ones are true (T) and which ones are false (F).

I. In India, various kinds of harassment, exploitation and violence are common against women.

II. In gender division, unequal roles are assigned by the society to men and women.

III. Gandhiji believed that politics must be guided by ethics drawn from religion.

IV. The most important aspect of the caste inequality is untouchability.

Codes

	I	II	III	IV		I	II	III	IV
(a)	T	T	T	T	(b)	T	T	T	F
(c)	T	F	T	F	(d)	F	F	T	T

Darken your choice with HB Pencil

1. ⓐ ⓑ ⓒ ⓓ	10. ⓐ ⓑ ⓒ ⓓ	19. ⓐ ⓑ ⓒ ⓓ	28. ⓐ ⓑ ⓒ ⓓ	37. ⓐ ⓑ ⓒ ⓓ	46. ⓐ ⓑ ⓒ ⓓ
2. ⓐ ⓑ ⓒ ⓓ	11. ⓐ ⓑ ⓒ ⓓ	20. ⓐ ⓑ ⓒ ⓓ	29. ⓐ ⓑ ⓒ ⓓ	38. ⓐ ⓑ ⓒ ⓓ	47. ⓐ ⓑ ⓒ ⓓ
3. ⓐ ⓑ ⓒ ⓓ	12. ⓐ ⓑ ⓒ ⓓ	21. ⓐ ⓑ ⓒ ⓓ	30. ⓐ ⓑ ⓒ ⓓ	39. ⓐ ⓑ ⓒ ⓓ	48. ⓐ ⓑ ⓒ ⓓ
4. ⓐ ⓑ ⓒ ⓓ	13. ⓐ ⓑ ⓒ ⓓ	22. ⓐ ⓑ ⓒ ⓓ	31. ⓐ ⓑ ⓒ ⓓ	40. ⓐ ⓑ ⓒ ⓓ	49. ⓐ ⓑ ⓒ ⓓ
5. ⓐ ⓑ ⓒ ⓓ	14. ⓐ ⓑ ⓒ ⓓ	23. ⓐ ⓑ ⓒ ⓓ	32. ⓐ ⓑ ⓒ ⓓ	41. ⓐ ⓑ ⓒ ⓓ	50. ⓐ ⓑ ⓒ ⓓ
6. ⓐ ⓑ ⓒ ⓓ	15. ⓐ ⓑ ⓒ ⓓ	24. ⓐ ⓑ ⓒ ⓓ	33. ⓐ ⓑ ⓒ ⓓ	42. ⓐ ⓑ ⓒ ⓓ	
7. ⓐ ⓑ ⓒ ⓓ	16. ⓐ ⓑ ⓒ ⓓ	25. ⓐ ⓑ ⓒ ⓓ	34. ⓐ ⓑ ⓒ ⓓ	43. ⓐ ⓑ ⓒ ⓓ	
8. ⓐ ⓑ ⓒ ⓓ	17. ⓐ ⓑ ⓒ ⓓ	26. ⓐ ⓑ ⓒ ⓓ	35. ⓐ ⓑ ⓒ ⓓ	44. ⓐ ⓑ ⓒ ⓓ	
9. ⓐ ⓑ ⓒ ⓓ	18. ⓐ ⓑ ⓒ ⓓ	27. ⓐ ⓑ ⓒ ⓓ	36. ⓐ ⓑ ⓒ ⓓ	45. ⓐ ⓑ ⓒ ⓓ	

Answer Sheet

Chapter 01

1. (c) 2. (c) 3. (a) 4. (b) 5. (b) 6. (d) 7. (b) 8. (d) 9. (b) 10. (b)
11. (b) 12. (a) 13. (b) 14. (a) 15. (a) 16. (c) 17. (d) 18. (a) 19. (c) 20. (c)
21. (b) 22. (b) 23. (c) 24. (d) 25. (a)

Chapter 02

1. (b) 2. (a) 3. (a) 4. (b) 5. (a) 6. (c) 7. (d) 8. (b) 9. (c) 10. (a)
11. (c) 12. (d) 13. (d) 14. (b) 15. (d) 16. (b) 17. (d) 18. (c) 19. (c) 20. (c)
21. (b) 22. (d) 23. (b) 24. (c) 25. (a) 26. (c) 27. (a)

Chapter 03

1. (b) 2. (d) 3. (c) 4. (b) 5. (c) 6. (b) 7. (c) 8. (b) 9. (a) 10. (b)
11. (b) 12. (a) 13. (b) 14. (c) 15. (b) 16. (b) 17. (d) 18. (c) 19. (a) 20. (c)
21. (d) 22. (b) 23. (b) 24. (b) 25. (c) 26. (a) 27. (b)

Chapter 04

1. (c) 2. (a) 3. (b) 4. (b) 5. (d) 6. (c) 7. (a) 8. (b) 9. (c) 10. (c)
11. (b) 12. (a) 13. (d) 14. (c) 15. (b) 16. (d) 17. (c) 18. (b) 19. (b) 20. (d)
21. (b) 22. (c) 23. (a) 24. (a) 25. (b) 26. (a) 27. (b)

Chapter 05

1. (d) 2. (d) 3. (b) 4. (c) 5. (a) 6. (c) 7. (c) 8. (a) 9. (d) 10. (b)
11. (c) 12. (c) 13. (d) 14. (d) 15. (c) 16. (d) 17. (b) 18. (c) 19. (a) 20. (a)
21. (b) 22. (b) 23. (d) 24. (b) 25. (a)

Chapter 06

1. (a) 2. (a) 3. (c) 4. (b) 5. (d) 6. (a) 7. (c) 8. (c) 9. (c) 10. (b)
11. (a) 12. (c) 13. (d) 14. (c) 15. (d) 16. (d) 17. (c) 18. (a) 19. (d) 20. (a)
21. (d) 22. (d) 23. (a) 24. (d) 25. (b)

Chapter 07

1. (d) 2. (c) 3. (c) 4. (a) 5. (d) 6. (d) 7. (c) 8. (d) 9. (a) 10. (a)
11. (c) 12. (c) 13. (d) 14. (c) 15. (d) 16. (d) 17. (d) 18. (c) 19. (c) 20. (d)
21. (a) 22. (c) 23. (a) 24. (a) 25. (b) 26. (d) 27. (b) 28. (a)

Chapter 08

1. (d)	**2.** (d)	**3.** (d)	**4.** (b)	**5.** (d)	**6.** (d)	**7.** (d)	**8.** (d)	**9.** (a)	**10.** (d)
11. (c)	**12.** (a)	**13.** (d)	**14.** (a)	**15.** (a)	**16.** (d)	**17.** (d)	**18.** (c)	**19.** (c)	**20.** (b)
21. (d)	**22.** (c)	**23.** (a)	**24.** (b)	**25.** (b)					

Chapter 09

1. (d)	**2.** (d)	**3.** (d)	**4.** (d)	**5.** (d)	**6.** (a)	**7.** (c)	**8.** (c)	**9.** (b)	**10.** (b)
11. (b)	**12.** (c)	**13.** (d)	**14.** (d)	**15.** (c)	**16.** (d)	**17.** (c)	**18.** (a)	**19.** (c)	**20.** (a)
21. (d)	**22.** (d)	**23.** (b)	**24.** (b)	**25.** (c)	**26.** (a)	**27.** (c)	**28.** (a)	**29.** (b)	**30.** (a)

Chapter 10

1. (c)	**2.** (d)	**3.** (d)	**4.** (c)	**5.** (a)	**6.** (c)	**7.** (c)	**8.** (d)	**9.** (d)	**10.** (d)
11. (c)	**12.** (d)	**13.** (a)	**14.** (d)	**15.** (c)	**16.** (c)	**17.** (d)	**18.** (b)	**19.** (d)	**20.** (a)
21. (a)									

Chapter 11

1. (b)	**2.** (a)	**3.** (b)	**4.** (b)	**5.** (d)	**6.** (c)	**7.** (c)	**8.** (d)	**9.** (a)	**10.** (c)
11. (a)	**12.** (b)	**13.** (d)	**14.** (a)	**15.** (d)	**16.** (b)	**17.** (b)	**18.** (b)	**19.** (d)	**20.** (a)
21. (b)	**22.** (a)	**23.** (d)	**24.** (b)	**25.** (a)	**26.** (b)	**27.** (c)	**28.** (b)	**29.** (c)	

Chapter 12

1. (c)	**2.** (b)	**3.** (c)	**4.** (c)	**5.** (a)	**6.** (c)	**7.** (a)	**8.** (c)	**9.** (d)	**10.** (b)
11. (d)	**12.** (a)	**13.** (d)	**14.** (b)	**15.** (a)	**16.** (c)	**17.** (a)	**18.** (d)	**19.** (b)	**20.** (d)
21. (c)	**22.** (a)	**23.** (a)	**24.** (b)						

Chapter 13

1. (a)	**2.** (b)	**3.** (a)	**4.** (d)	**5.** (d)	**6.** (c)	**7.** (d)	**8.** (b)	**9.** (c)	**10.** (a)
11. (c)	**12.** (d)	**13.** (d)	**14.** (a)	**15.** (a)	**16.** (d)	**17.** (b)	**18.** (d)	**19.** (b)	**20.** (d)
21. (b)	**22.** (c)	**23.** (c)	**24.** (d)	**25.** (b)	**26.** (b)	**27.** (b)			

Chapter 14

1. (d)	**2.** (d)	**3.** (c)	**4.** (d)	**5.** (d)	**6.** (c)	**7.** (c)	**8.** (c)	**9.** (b)	**10.** (c)
11. (c)	**12.** (d)	**13.** (c)	**14.** (a)	**15.** (d)	**16.** (b)	**17.** (d)	**18.** (c)	**19.** (c)	**20.** (c)
21. (d)	**22.** (b)	**23.** (c)	**24.** (a)	**25.** (c)	**26.** (a)	**27.** (d)			

Chapter 15

1. (d)	**2.** (b)	**3.** (d)	**4.** (d)	**5.** (c)	**6.** (c)	**7.** (c)	**8.** (d)	**9.** (a)	**10.** (c)
11. (c)	**12.** (d)	**13.** (c)	**14.** (b)	**15.** (d)	**16.** (d)	**17.** (d)	**18.** (d)	**19.** (c)	**20.** (b)
21. (b)	**22.** (a)	**23.** (c)							

Chapter 16

1. (d)	2. (a)	3. (d)	4. (d)	5. (c)	6. (c)	7. (b)	8. (d)	9. (c)	10. (c)
11. (c)	12. (d)	13. (d)	14. (d)	15. (d)	16. (c)	17. (d)	18. (d)	19. (d)	20. (b)
21. (a)	22. (c)	23. (b)	24. (d)	25. (a)	26. (b)				

Chapter 17

1. (d)	2. (b)	3. (d)	4. (d)	5. (a)	6. (d)	7. (d)	8. (c)	9. (c)	10. (a)
11. (b)	12. (d)	13. (c)	14. (c)	15. (c)	16. (d)	17. (b)	18. (c)	19. (d)	20. (c)
21. (c)									

Practice Set 01

1. (b)	2. (d)	3. (d)	4. (b)	5. (b)	6. (a)	7. (d)	8. (d)	9. (a)	10. (b)
11. (c)	12. (a)	13. (d)	14. (d)	15. (d)	16. (d)	17. (b)	18. (d)	19. (c)	20. (c)
21. (d)	22. (d)	23. (a)	24. (d)	25. (b)	26. (d)	27. (a)	28. (d)	29. (c)	30. (d)
31. (d)	32. (d)	33. (c)	34. (d)	35. (a)	36. (a)	37. (d)	38. (c)	39. (a)	40. (b)
41. (a)	42. (a)	43. (b)	44. (d)	45. (a)	46. (c)	47. (a)	48. (d)	49. (a)	50. (c)

Practice Set 02

1. (b)	2. (d)	3. (a)	4. (b)	5. (a)	6. (b)	7. (b)	8. (c)	9. (d)	10. (d)
11. (c)	12. (a)	13. (a)	14. (d)	15. (d)	16. (d)	17. (b)	18. (a)	19. (a)	20. (a)
21. (b)	22. (a)	23. (c)	24. (b)	25. (d)	26. (a)	27. (a)	28. (d)	29. (c)	30. (c)
31. (a)	32. (a)	33. (b)	34. (b)	35. (a)	36. (b)	37. (d)	38. (c)	39. (d)	40. (a)
41. (d)	42. (b)	43. (a)	44. (a)	45. (a)	46. (b)	47. (d)	48. (a)	49. (d)	50. (a)

Practice Set 03

1. (c)	2. (a)	3. (c)	4. (a)	5. (d)	6. (d)	7. (a)	8. (a)	9. (d)	10. (b)
11. (b)	12. (b)	13. (d)	14. (b)	15. (b)	16. (c)	17. (c)	18. (b)	19. (d)	20. (d)
21. (a)	22. (c)	23. (d)	24. (b)	25. (c)	26. (a)	27. (a)	28. (c)	29. (d)	30. (a)
31. (b)	32. (b)	33. (c)	34. (a)	35. (d)	36. (c)	37. (a)	38. (c)	39. (b)	40. (a)
41. (a)	42. (a)	43. (b)	44. (d)	45. (a)	46. (b)	47. (a)	48. (c)	49. (b)	50. (a)